"Stay Out of Politics"

Ronald Aronson

"Stay Out of Politics"

A Philosopher Views South Africa

The University of Chicago Press   Chicago and London

Ronald Aronson, who studied with Herbert Marcuse, is
professor of humanities at the Weekend College, Wayne
State University. His book *Sartre's Second Critique* is also
published by the University of Chicago Press.

The University of Chicago Press, Ltd., London
© 1990 by The University of Chicago
All rights reserved. Published 1990
Printed in the United States of America

99 98 97 96 95 94 93 92 91 90   54321

Library of Congress Cataloging-in-Publication Data

Aronson, Ronald, 1938–
  "Stay out of politics."

  Includes bibliographical references.
    1. South Africa—Politics and government—1978–
2. Race relations—South Africa.   3. Apartheid—South
Africa.   I. Title.
DT1945.A76   1990   305.8′00968   89–20291
ISBN 0–226–02801–1   (alk. paper)
ISBN 0–226–02803–8 (pbk. :   alk. paper)

⊗ The paper used in this publication meets
the minimum requirements of the American National
Standard for Information Sciences—Permanence of
Paper for Printed Library Materials, ANSI Z39.48-1984.

Contents

v

Preface: A Philosopher in South Africa

The last thing that I expected was to love South Africa. The trip promised to be difficult, beginning with deciding to go, a decision so much against the grain of political and personal common sense. I anticipated difficulty in teaching, uncomfortable personal confrontations, trying moral and political choices. But, after all, the greatest strains came afterward, upon returning home. Some of these homecoming problems are not surprising. Anyone would have to make serious adjustments on returning from being an honored guest to being an ordinary person, or on landing from an intense interlude having a single focus back into usual routines and daily cares. And it is not surprising that one might have difficulty returning from a revolutionary situation where everything seems possible to a society where, even in the presidential season, almost no one speaks of real alternatives. And, although jarring at first, there is an obvious contrast between South Africa's overpowering moral and emotional clarity and the daily battle to steer through our confusing gray-on-gray world.

But, most unexpectedly of all, homecoming was painful because I had so quickly, and so intensely, come to love the people I met in South Africa. I loved them for their graciousness and charm, and because they readily shared their pain and struggles and hopes, and even their hatreds and weaknesses. White or black, they seemed a people of little artifice, a people who easily opened and gave themselves. Accordingly, my heart went out to South Africa, to South Africans. Coming home, I missed them intensely, and I still miss them.

What do these feelings, and the experience that generated them, have to do with philosophy? Many narratives have been written about South Africa, and will continue to be written, seeking to convey this or that person's individual experience of the world's most controversial, most suffering place. While such feelings may belong in these accounts, what can they possibly have to do with a philosopher's reflections? *Philosophical Forum* has published a special issue on apartheid (vol. 18, nos. 2–3, Winter–Spring 1987), which has been banned in South Africa; it explores such issues as the nature of apartheid ideology, the prospects for a post-apartheid society, the uses of language to legitimate the current illegitimate situation, moral justifications of sanctions and of violence in the struggle against apartheid, and the nature of racism.

For me to begin with love, and make it one of the main themes of this book, is equally philosophical. After all, philosophy begins with love. Most famously, in the *Symposium* and the *Republic* Plato focuses on the good as philosophy's central principle, arguing in the first dialogue that the good, reason's motivation and ultimate destination, is also the real object of all love. In the second he discusses at length the steps the philosopher must go through in order to reach the good, and in the Allegory of the Cave makes the pivotal act a conversion, an inclination of the soul away from the ordinary world and towards the good, a conversion which can never be motivated by reason alone.

If love for the good is Platonic philosophy's motivation, its guiding principle, and final destination, we may also recall the love for Athens that drove the historical Socrates, described in Plato's early dialogues, to his mission and his death. As the *Apology* and *Crito* make clear, the questions leading to philosophy spring from Socrates' deep feeling for Athens. First, he resolves to be its gadfly; then, sentenced but offered escape, he refuses to undermine Athens by fleeing its decree. This affective tie between Socrates and Athens gives rise to philosophy, prodding him to ask its initiating questions, such as, "What is piety?" and "What is virtue?" And at the end we see that this tie is also the first principle of his own being: better to die than redefine himself without Athens, a Socrates-out-of-Athens, a wandering Sophist selling his wares no matter where to no matter whom.

Behind Socrates' first steps and Plato's first full elaboration of reason, then, lie commitments, based on love, that give rise to reason but that reason alone can never explain. If philosophy's love of wisdom begins with a specific love for Athens, this love develops into a broader love for the world. Thus devoted, Plato set the course for philosophy, working towards bringing the good into the world, developing reason and using it to improve the human lot.

As the reader will see, my own tie with South Africa started from the opposite direction; not with love, but with hostility toward its social system that spilled over to all things South African. Like so many others, I could originally relate to the place only by keeping myself distant from the abhorrent apartheid system. Much of the narrative part of what follows tells the story of my becoming more and more deeply involved with South Africa. Without being a citizen, then, and after a sort of conversion to be described below, in my own way I still follow the Socratic inspiration: philosophizing out of love for the place.

Most American philosophers, like most South African philosophers, are professionally indifferent to what goes on in South Africa today. Whatever may be their personal commitments, professionally they have no difficulty staying out of politics. A brief tour through the program and abstracts of a randomly selected issue of the *Proceedings and Addresses of the American Philosophical Association* will turn up a handful of topics that are directly social and political, a slightly larger handful that are indirectly related, and nothing on South Africa. Sadly enough, this seems to be true in South Africa as well. The 1986 and 1987 volumes of *Philosophical Papers,* a South African journal whose editors "regard the policy of apartheid as an infringement of human, civil and academic rights, and an affront to human dignity," have been unable to present a single article focusing on apartheid, and only two or three (out of thirty) on social or political topics. Questions about the current social, political, and economic landscape of apartheid are probably less pertinent to the teaching and practice of philosophy today than they are to the teaching and practice of, say, literary criticism or (to venture beyond the liberal arts) to the teaching and practice of engineering.

Today it is necessary, then, to bring Plato into the present, and I begin by affirming my belief that philosophy not only "has a role to play" but that it can, and must, involve itself in the vital social and political issues of our time. To discuss how this philosopher involved himself means saying something about the philosophy through which this book encounters South Africa. One could, and indeed should, ask about the presuppositions behind any discussion of South Africa, but nowhere do premises play as important a role as in a philosopher's work. Indeed, if they are more central here, it is because of the very nature of a philosopher's account; it will not so much offer new information as a perspective, or a series of related perspectives, for viewing South Africa. Like any, they cannot help but be personal perspectives and, like any, they can be expected to be coherent, clear, grounded, and conscious. But if they are a philosopher's, they will show South Africa through certain lenses, pose certain types of questions about South Africa, set South Africa in certain contexts, reflect on South Africa and frame it according to certain interests.

Then what are they, this philosopher's lenses, questions, contexts, and interests? I wish it were as easy, at the outset, as applying a few labels: a rationalist inspired by Socrates and Plato, a Marcusean Marxist concerned about the relationship of theory to practice, a Sartrean concerned about how individual responsibility and social reality converge, a feminist concerned with the intersection of personal experience and objective structures, a philosopher of the Holocaust and of history seeking to rescue hope from the maelstrom of the twentieth century. I claim each of these labels as my own—each reflects an important stage of my formation and plane of my encounter with South Africa—but such labeling is also grossly inadequate. What really does each of these labels, or perspectives, mean? How do I relate each to the others—through a kind of additive eclecticism in which the real force of each becomes diluted? I have not tried simply to gather these perspectives together by diminishing each of them by the others (and so weakening their force). Rather, in my work and outlook I have sought to preserve what I regard as each perspective's fundamental thrust, not set alongside the others but actively deepened by them.

The conception of reason suggested at the beginning of this preface was developed in my studies with Herbert Marcuse. At its core, reason is not a neutral or a merely intellectual or a purely technical faculty; it springs from an existential engagement, its passion for grasping and realizing the good. When I was a graduate student, the single lecture of Marcuse that left the most lasting impression on me dealt with historical objectivity. He stressed that reason was committed from the beginning to the amelioration of the struggle for survival. Every society disposes over certain capacities for ameliorating the struggle, capacities whose use can be rationally, and objectively, evaluated. Other, more limited, and even contrary, conceptions of reason are certainly thinkable, just as it might be possible to "rationally" discuss destroying the planet.

But such discussions, like Herman Kahn's *Thinking the Unthinkable,* about nuclear war, mean violating the underlying tie of reason to the pursuit of the best possible human existence: much "rational" thought is the calculus of an uprooted and irrational reason. At root, reason presupposes a value, a commitment to a larger community and, indeed, a certain set of feelings. Other kinds of, and uses of, reason may be possible, but they reflect other choices, other projects, that must be combated even if they are not worth discussing.

If reason cannot be understood apart from love, neither can it be separated from politics. Plato's effort at integration established the philosophical tradition within which this book has been written. This tradition is the framework within which my own decision to go to South Africa was made. Having such a commitment, I could scarcely resist the opportunity to practice philosophy in South Africa.

I speak of "practicing" philosophy. Even before I went, the personal decision to go involved me in trying to decide what was the right course to take—to boycott South Africa or to engage with it. As soon as I began lecturing there, I discovered South Africa to be a society where there is far less of a separation between theory and practice than in the United States. Ideas matter, thought and dialogue have consequences because reality is open to change. I also found it to be a society that imposes questions about how to experience social reality: above all, what is the relationship of direct personal experience, and the feelings inseparable from it, to reflection on the thousand and one ambiguities which surround it (and with which people try so hard to surround it)?

Visiting South Africa for five weeks in August and September, 1987, in the midst of the state of emergency, during the largest miners' strike ever, and in the wake of student disruptions of the visit to the University of Cape Town by Conor Cruise O'Brien, I found it to be a society gripped by, and living through, every major issue I had planned to lecture about. One of my themes was hope: encounters with the democratic movement in a period of ebb and fierce repression drove me to ask about the frailty, and resiliency, of hope in South Africa. Another of my themes was the idea and reality of progress: it was impossible to talk about it without taking into account that I was in Africa, and that my black students were still its victims and objects. And I found myself unable to visit townships without seeing, and reflecting on, the negative consequences of such progress. Nor could I think about progress as technical development without asking my African and "colored" students at the University of the Western Cape how they would weigh the newly opened Du Toit's Kloof tunnel against other possible kinds of progress. Similarly, lecturing on the explosive social irrationality of Hitler's Germany and Stalin's Soviet Union at a time of the spectacular rise of South Africa's Conservative party into the role of official opposition, could I avoid asking about the irrationality of apartheid? Having wrestled with the question of individual responsibility for social evil, I could scarcely avoid asking whites who hated apartheid but who went along with it and opposed the United Democratic Front about *their* complicity in today's South Africa.

Accordingly, the pages that follow present this philosopher's encounter with South Africa. The introduction describes the issues raised, and the process involved, in my deciding to go. Part 1, the next two chapters, recounts my impressions of South Africa, first of lecturing there, then of my various encounters with the effects of apartheid. Each of these chapters is roughly chronological, the second less so than the first. The reader will notice that I am describing two rather different but overlapping experiences, of performing the professional function for which I was invited to South Africa, and of experiencing, from the peculiar distance of a white academic visitor, various aspects of apartheid. Part 2 presents two of my many interactions with South Africa, both of which were originally written and presented while I was there. The first began as a lecture directed to English-speaking whites who oppose apartheid, "but"—that is, they resist accepting, and working on behalf of, majority rule. It raises the question of individual responsibility for an evil social system, and was meant as a provocation. The second, a lecture originally directed to anti-apartheid activists, focuses on the meaning and nature of hope in the kind of difficult times faced by the democratic movement in South Africa, and was meant as a consolation.

The final section presents my reflections on South Africa since my return. It returns to some of the many ambiguities I had shelved while initially encountering apartheid, complexities that will cast a shadow across the free South Africa of the future but that do not lessen the urgent case for majority rule. The first of these two chapters focuses on white South Africa; the second on the movement for majority rule.

Each of the three parts following the introduction is thus written in a slightly different register, passing from personal experience to engaged argument, and then to analysis and reflection. The three voices, overlapping in any case, are intended to complement each other; in moving from one to the next, I try to build towards a single understanding of South Africa today.

This book is informed by a sense of fear for many of the people I talked with, a fear made all the stronger by the fact that I was invited specifically to present a memorial lecture at the University of Natal for political philosopher and anti-apartheid activist Rick Turner, who was assassinated in 1978. The reader will understand that the police-state conditions in which the opposition lives make it impossible to use people's names or clearly convey their identities. This book is marked by my dread that, in spite of the inevitability that "apartheid will go," the ruling whites may provoke a catastrophe by their insistence on continuing to control black lives even while claiming to reform apartheid;[1] and that those on the right, with or without state connivance, are actively undertaking to bring the whole society to ruin rather than accept majority rule. Since my visit, organizations I will mention below, such as the South African National Students Congress (SANSCO), the End Conscription Campaign (ECC) and even the United Democratic Front (UDF) have statutorily been "restricted"—barred from all political activity; the headquarters of anti-apartheid organizations have been bombed; detentions have continued; hundreds of people have been murdered in township political violence and in the bloody conflict in Natal between Inkatha and those loyal to the UDF.[2] Specific individuals have been targeted by vigilantes. In the words of a report entitled "Repression and the State of Emergency, June 1987 to March 1989," "assassinations have the effect of controlling government opposition when all other methods, such as detention or intimidation, have failed."[3]

The author of this report, social anthropologist and leading white anti-apartheid activist, David Webster, was murdered as this manuscript was being prepared for publication. While I was in South Africa I spent an evening and a morning with him, which I will describe in the postscript. He was shot on May Day 1989, in a well-planned operation carried out by an apparently highly trained team, as he went to let his dogs out of his car in front of his house. He died immediately. His funeral became the occasion for the largest anti-apartheid demonstration for many months under the state of emergency. Anti-apartheid activists suspected police complicity and predicted that, like Rick Turner's killer, David Webster's murderers would probably never be found.

In this book I have tried to convey my fear and dread about the fate of people like David, who showed me, and have shown the world, their awe-inspiring energy and courage, their spirit of struggle and self-sacrifice, their capacity for humor and solidarity, and above all—amazingly—their continuing commitment to a nonracial future. I dedicate this book to them, and especially to the memory of David Webster.

I would like to thank the Universities of Natal, Durban-Westville, the Western Cape, Cape Town, and Stellenbosch, as well as all of my friends in South Africa. Phyllis Aronson discovered them with me. Special thanks to Raphael and Elizabeth de Kadt, Andrew Nash, Roslyn and William Holderness, Lungisile Ntsebeza, Mala and Prem Singh, Mohammed and Sara Seedat, Maggie Friedman, Gary Lubner, Karin Schreiber, Ian Phillips, Gillian Woods, Michael Lang, Willem Landman, André Du Toit, Mervyn and Lola Frost, Graham Tyndall, Christopher Ballantine, Angus Stewart, Valerie Broin, Leonard Suransky, Helen Samberg, Saul Wellman, Pamela Aronson, Robert Paul Wolff, and Steve Golin.

Introduction: Deciding to Go

The meeting opened stiffly, formally, but with scrupulous attention to democratic procedures. The convener (who was detained briefly by the security police two weeks later) asked for someone to chair and, receiving no volunteers, went from person to person until one of the comrades accepted. This young man, appearing no older than eighteen, stated that they had been called together to inquire into the visit of the American Prof in relation to the boycott and would begin by posing a few questions to him. These young people shared a belief that South Africa's universities fell under a wider ban imposed, at the request of the ANC, by the rest of the world on South African culture.

Without hesitation another young man raised his hand and asked the question that was foremost on everyone's mind. "Will the Prof explain why he did not honor the boycott?" His steely assurance almost made me feel on trial. I looked around at the dozen young black men and women who had been waiting and the two young white men who had accompanied me into the room. Everyone awaited my answer. It was a tense moment.

During the past two days I had been told that I was in danger of having my opening lecture disrupted. The mood among the young black comrades was surly, especially in light of the recent events at Cape Town, where Conor Cruise O'Brien[1] had publicly defied the boycott and provoked a near-explosion on campus. Foreign lecturers were inviting, perhaps irresistible, targets, especially given the widespread if vague sense that a boycott was going on. When I originally heard about this, I thought of inviting students to interrupt. I would gladly devote the first several minutes of my Hiroshima Day lecture to answering questions about who I was, why I had come to South Africa, and my attitude towards the boycott.

As it turned out, I was fortunate not to have that lecture disrupted. It would not have gone so easily for me. The actual encounter, immediately after my first public lecture, was to take over an hour, in a very strained atmosphere, and involve every aspect of my trip. The great danger for someone in my position, I was later told, was to respond in an irritable or defensive manner. A hostile confrontation could easily make the professor the butt of a spontaneous student movement—led by these officers and members of the Black Students Society, affiliate of the South African National Student Congress (SANSCO)—which would totally sabotage the purpose of my visit.

The invitation had come two years earlier, and had been in the offing for a year before that: Would I be the lecturer for the Students' Visiting Lectureship Trust Fund in Political Philosophy at the University of Natal, Durban? On August 1, 1987, my wife, Phyllis, and I left Detroit on the evening flight to London, the first leg of a trip which would take me to lecture at five universities and before a number of groups in Durban, Cape Town, and Johannesburg.

Go to South Africa? A South African political philosopher I met in London in 1984 at the home of a well-known Marxist sociologist posed the possibility of my visiting to lecture for several weeks. Although I was impressed by my colleague's commitment to the struggle against apartheid, and I treated his proposal with interest, it first seemed as if it had come from another planet. Avoiding lobster tails, fruit, and all things South African had come to be a moral-political ritual. The anti-apartheid climate in London reinforced my own hostility. A white psychologist I later met in Durban, one who happens also to be an anti-apartheid activist, talked about visiting a peer organization in London at the same time and being met with instant rejection upon telling them she was from South Africa. After a brief, embarrassed emergency conference, they concluded that they could not only not talk to a white South African but could not even sell her their literature. I received the same sort of reaction when I told the sociologist's son I had been invited. A bright young political activist, he erupted briefly about South Africa: Was I a supporter of apartheid? The boycott must not be broken for any reason!

In the face of such resistance, I took over two years to make the decision. At first the idea seemed morally, politically, and personally absurd. And yet the thought of visiting South Africa at the invitation of a radical colleague whose purpose for staying there was to help the struggle for majority rule, was intriguing. Over the months my objections to going began to dissolve or be satisfied, and the reasons for going grew stronger and more insistent. Each personal layer of resistance I overcame raised, and resolved, more general issues about how to approach South Africa. In the process, this archetypal land of evil, deserving to be shunned in every way, slowly took shape before me as the real place it is, whose vast majority bitterly opposes apartheid and includes thousands of progressive whites, like myself, who are committed to majority rule and deeply involved in the struggle to achieve it. In telling this story of how I came to engage with them, I am also making an argument against the all too common posture, originally my own as well, that keeps South Africa, and South Africans, at arm's length, avoiding them like the plague even in the guise of seeking to help them.

I was to hear echoes of the young activist's reaction, of the Durban psychologist's experience, of my own initial sense of the absurdity of visiting South Africa many times while I was deciding and then planning to make the trip. Usually nothing very definite. "South Africa?" Always with a quizzical brow, as if I were talking about visiting that run-down house on the block that the whole neighborhood had decided was too strange to go near, the family too unlike the rest of us, perhaps queer or sinister, to be considered part of the same human race. The tone said: "Why on earth would anyone ever want to go *there?*"

Unlike virtually any other of the world's tormented but still accessible places, South Africa is a country "we" have decided to keep our distance from. Sophisticated liberals and radicals will visit Nicaragua, say, or Israel, the West Bank and Gaza, and will engage actively with these places. But in the culture I inhabit, except for a handful of Africanists, no one goes to South Africa. South Africa is stained by a fundamental moral pollution for which the recommended politics is also a kind of hygiene: to keep away.

A letter-writer to the *New York Times* argues, for example, that "the essential issue with respect to sanctions against South Africa [is] that it is immoral on our part to profit from slave labor and to assist governments and entrepreneurs to profit from it, regardless of whether or not the sanctions are of immediate or long-range benefit to either of the parties." In other words, our real concern should not be to arrogantly decide what is good for black South Africa but to stop being "part of an abhorrent system." Morality demands a rupture with our practice of feeding off the evil that is apartheid.[2]

This is a strong argument, and I would suggest that its moral premise, as much as any political logic, explains why we easily embrace the idea of boycotts, embargoes, and disinvestment. Yet it is worth noting in response that there has been no American campaign to support the African National Congress similar to the remarkably successful efforts on behalf of the Nicaraguan contras, UNITA in Angola, the mujadeen in Afghanistan, or Renamo in Mozambique. I would suggest that this is because the political goal of many anti-apartheid support groups outside South Africa has not been to physically overthrow the minority state but to promote their own governments' and economies' withdrawal from South Africa as a form of pressure. What they seem to be saying by this is that apartheid is evil but so is violence; rupturing with the apartheid system is a purely good act, a moral act which does not implicate itself in any sort of evil. The same cannot be said for directly assisting those trying to physically overthrow its rulers.

In other words, one source of the current campaigns is an understandable, and laudable, desire to break with evil. But it easily leads us to completely wash our hands of South Africa. My own thoughts began to move in a somewhat different direction. Caring about South Africa, I began to think, may mean not only adhering to the position of the African National Congress advocating disinvestment and sanctions but also more actively and directly engaging with the country in a variety of ways—even perhaps by going there.

My colleague kept writing to me after my return from London to Detroit, and so South Africa continued tugging at me. Perhaps it was my commitment to keep alive the hopes of the 1960s, especially in the dispiriting 1980s, but I found it impossible to close the door on the chance to connect with the movement for change inside South Africa. Everything I had been thinking, writing and doing for twenty years led me toward, rather than away from, encountering apartheid.

The official invitation, from the vice-chancellor of the University of Natal, came while I was still of two minds. As I thought of saying no, to make my own protest against apartheid, I remembered the days when friends and relatives avoided buying German cars because of the Holocaust, and then when some even stopped buying American cars because of Vietnam. These were private protests, not designed to effect change, but operating as acts of personal dissociation. The invitation forced the final step of seeing South Africa in the same light as any other place. Not, How can I dissociate myself from this evil? but, How can I oppose it effectively? It was time for me to extend to South Africa the conclusions I had drawn from studying Jean-Paul Sartre's efforts to decide what one does with one's dirty hands.

I agree that political action usually is, and should be, rooted in the kind of moral outrage expressed by the writer to the *New York Times* quoted above. He or she is obviously concerned about doing the right thing and refuses to be associated with, or profit from, an evil system. But this is also the kind of argument given by Lucien Drelitsch, proponent of an idealist and purist revolutionary morality, in Sartre's screenplay *In the Mesh*, and by Hugo, assassin of Hoederer, in *Dirty Hands*. In these works Sartre is exploring a fundamental philosophical issue, criticizing a moralism that insists we act as we ought to act (as the letter writer insisted), regardless of the consequences.

Sartre accuses this moralism, or idealism, of tacitly sanctioning, partaking of, and benefiting from the evils it would pretend to steer clear of. He charges its posture of moral purity with neglecting other, more systematic oppressions and with being politically ineffective. In *The Devil and the Good Lord*, after depicting disaster raining down on the peasants because of Goetz's ahistorical and unsocial—in other words, abstract—efforts to do good, Sartre develops instead a dialectical vision. He accepts the reality of violence and inhumanity everywhere around and within us, and, without pretending that we can ever have clean hands, he urges us towards sustained political struggle rather than moral statement; joining forces with others rather than acting as isolated individuals. Our goal should be to overcome the tension between a moral but abstract commitment on the one hand and an insistence on realism and effectiveness divorced from its original moral goals on the other. At the end of *The Devil and the Good Lord* Sartre calls for active political involvement using all the weapons at one's disposal, not pretending that one can get through this life with unsoiled hands. Goetz transcends the moralism of Hugo and Lucien by moving on to a mature and responsible—and realistic—commitment to politics. He gives up the demand for immediate liberation, as well as *the need to be good,* and accepts being a leader in a prolonged struggle.[3]

For me, the lesson of this, one of the richest of Sartrean lines of thought, led to the simple question: How might my South African comrades best make use of me? First, obviously, I was in no position to make a gesture that might attract enough notice to make any political difference. But my presence there might have a very small positive effect. Second, it made no sense to shun those who invited me and those who might hear me talk. I began to be irritated by the purist logic of those outside South Africa who accept the ANC position on disinvestment and sanctions and regard anti-apartheid South African whites who stay and contribute as moral lepers, while welcoming and respecting as moral those who emigrate. (Within South Africa, I was to learn, blacks and anti-apartheid whites are deeply critical of those whites who have "taken the easy option" and emigrated. And they are quite contemptuous of those who have recently been frantically trying to acquire a second passport to thereby gain increased mobility. The worst among such whites, I was told, are those who join an anti-apartheid professional organization just before leaving—in order to acquire the right credentials in exile.) While pro-apartheid academic and political visitors come through South Africa all the time, and are prominently paraded before the public, the purist logic withholds our support from the very people who need it most, those who oppose apartheid and remain in the country. In the words of one colleague at Natal, effective politics means "isolating the regime, not the people." The question is, What will help change the situation?

Accordingly, I started asking about specific conditions of a possible visit. The questions reflected my own lack of knowledge of the current situation. Above all, would I be able to lecture to blacks as well as whites? In integrated settings? And without censorship? Thus began the first of many phone calls between Detroit and Durban. The University of Natal, as my colleague explained, is an autonomous state university operating on the British model. The statutes mandating a racial-admissions policy are left unenforced, as the state accedes to the university's insistence on admitting students solely according to academic qualifications. Moreover, the university houses black students on campus, in defiance of the Group Areas Act.[4] Natal's medical school, a mile away, was intended as South Africa's only black medical school, but the remainder of the university is said to be effectively nonracial,[5] with an enrollment that by 1988 would be nearly 30 percent African.[6] My colleague assured me that I would be quite free to explore any questions I wished in any way that I wished. Certainly South Africans are subjected to censorship under the Publications Act of 1974, and each week a new list of banned publications is circulated.[7] But banned books are widely used for academic purposes, banned materials are freely duplicated and handed out in the classrooms, and there is widespread discussion of banned organizations and individuals—all of which is rigorously defended by the English-language universities.

As the idea of a trip began to seem plausible, I slowly faced the most powerful positive reason for going: I had been invited. I expected difficulties, perhaps even conflict and pain, but South Africa drew me to it little by little, more and more powerfully. Not because I knew that my own specific work on Sartre and on the twentieth century would necessarily be important for students of social philosophy in South Africa. Indeed, I knew that I would hardly be the first foreign lecturer to bring radical ideas and a foreign anti-apartheid perspective to white and black students and staff. (In fact my visit would generate discussion between student organizations and academic staff about the best ways for communicating between themselves about inviting foreign visitors; by doing so, I was later told, my visit may have helped to clarify both the general question and the specific procedures of the academic boycott. If so, in the future, greater numbers of sympathetic foreign academics may be encouraged to visit South Africa.) My real motive was not to bear enlightenment to South Africa but rather solidarity. I felt drawn to interact with people whom I considered, in advance, as comrades; to learn, as much as to teach, but above all to involve myself with them.

I was becoming convinced. But what about the boycott? I now had to face this tangled question directly. Even if I personally saw a value in my going, could I violate a general position of the democratic movement in South Africa, of the African National Congress, and of the anti-apartheid movement overseas? Even if I disagreed with the position, a strategy is effective to the extent that it is followed. Breaking it only serves to demoralize the movement. Beyond being determined to keep solidarity with the South African anti-apartheid movement at home and in exile, I knew that it would make no sense to go to South Africa if the very act of going destroyed my credibility there. If I was perceived as violating the boycott, I would be shut out by the very people I wanted to spend time with.

Yet the more I explored, the more I wondered: Was there actually a boycott? And if so, who had imposed it? British faculty and student associations had certainly called for a boycott, but I could find nothing parallel in the United States. My own organization, the American Association of University Professors, had requested no such action from its members. While I was reflecting on such issues, the *Chronicle of Higher Education* published an article about the academic boycott. It was the report of an interview in Harare, Zimbabwe, with members of the leadership of the African National Congress. It turned out in this smallest of worlds that I knew the reporter, and I soon phoned him in Harare for confirmation of the impression he gave in the article, namely, that the ANC position was purposefully ambiguous. He said that in effect the boycott had become a selective one: go if your visit does not benefit apartheid or "apartheid universities" and especially if it can benefit the democratic movement. Computer experts whose work is used by the military and the state should definitely not go, but this would not apply to philosophers whose lectures might make a "progressive" contribution. Academic exchanges and new programs should be cleared by groups associated with the democratic movement. And any visit that benefits the state should be avoided. As a self-consciously nonracial university, Natal did not seem to me to fit the designation of "apartheid university." And, although I only found this out later, its Academic Staff Association and local chapter of the National Union of South African Students (NUSAS), the student organization that leads the university's Student Representative Council (SRC), are both affiliates of the United Democratic Front (UDF).

I had discussions with other people and groups in the United States who had been actively campaigning against apartheid and was encouraged to go on the grounds that my visit would be appropriate and perhaps even helpful for anti-apartheid activists at home. But this wouldn't get me into South Africa. Having decided to go, I had now to obtain a visa.

Several days after applying, I was surprised by a telephone call from the South African consulate in Chicago. The officer informed me that she was in charge of deciding whether to refer my application to Pretoria. After a few niceties she abruptly came to the point.

"Let me tell you what we're worried about, Professor Aronson. We're afraid that you might make political statements about South Africa while you're there."

I was taken aback by her directness. "I'm really not an expert on South Africa. I've been invited to lecture about areas in which I have considerable expertise, and I intend to speak only about questions that I've studied. I hope to learn about South Africa by going there."

"But who is Jean-Paul Sartre? Isn't he political?"

I had published two books about Sartre. "Certainly he wrote some political essays, but above all he's considered a philosopher. His fifty volumes include works of philosophy, fiction, theater, biographies, autobiography, critical and aesthetic essays."

"I see that you're invited by the Department of Political Science."

"Yes. As a social philosopher and historian of ideas." And I proceeded to describe the main areas of my interest. I talked in detail about the Holocaust and Stalinism, and then about the internal tensions within the idea of progress and their relevance to the twentieth century. As I spoke, I realized, for the first time in my life, that it might be a good idea to be boring. After a while I could tell by the silence at the other end that she was listening politely but paying no attention.

She let me finish, showing what I now know to be typical South African courtesy, but it was clear that she had long since stopped listening. "I will take all of this into consideration and let you know our decision tomorrow. Can you phone back tomorrow afternoon?"

I did. After her questioning of me the day before, I was surprised to find that she needed reminding who I was. Then she once again came right to the point. "We've decided to take a chance on you." And then after a brief conversation she once more brought up the key issue, concluding on a cautionary note: "Remember! Stay out of politics!"

The day my passport was returned with the visa stamped in it I realized that I still had to leap one more hurdle. I decided that I had to initiate one last contact with South Africa before my trip could become real, a contact with the African National Congress. In spite of all of the steps I had already taken, I knew that I couldn't go if they opposed my trip. Fundamentally, it was a question of being welcomed to South Africa by South African blacks, those with whom I wished to demonstrate my solidarity. Everyone in the world knows that *their* loyalty, overwhelmingly, is neither to people like my colleague at Natal nor to the state structure represented by the consular official, but to the ANC. But what would I say? Would I ask for their permission to lecture in South Africa? This seemed absurd, because it really was my decision to make and because it would only be burdening them with problems they certainly didn't need. But would I simply just phone their New York office to let them know I was going? If so, why call? Yet even if I felt unsure about what to say, it seemed absolutely necessary to inform them. A discussion with local political friends and with African-studies specialists who keep regular contact with the ANC produced the following idea: I would phone to let them know I was going, just to give them a sense of who I was, and to assure them that I intended to do nothing while in South Africa to show support for apartheid.

As it turned out, the woman I talked to at the New York office of the ANC had been to Detroit several months earlier, and I had met her at a reception where she spoke. In fact, she remembered me, because I had told her then that I had been invited to lecture in South Africa. I now conveyed my message, and she answered: "We'd like to talk with you when you come back." I suggested that I might phone from London and arrange to stop off in New York (in the end, the meeting never took place, because I was scheduled to pass through on a Sunday, when the ANC office is closed). And so we left off with: "I'll speak to you in September."

I was elated. I had been allowed into the country, and now I would carry with me the sense of being welcome. I was ready to go. More, I wanted to go.

Now, three months later, in South Africa, I was being confronted by the SANSCO students who were asserting *their* right to pass judgment on my visit. The officer at the consulate had told me to "stay out of politics." I was discovering abruptly that it would be impossible to avoid politics even if I wanted to. The success or failure of my trip hung in the balance. After this meeting I might be stamped as a reactionary and become fair game for protests and disruptions, as well as being avoided by people I wanted to meet. If so, I could foresee five frustrating weeks of being unable to make any more than polite, aloof contact with what I regarded as the real South Africa. Or, on the other hand, I would be regarded as acceptable.

I talked to them about my personal background, the reasons I had come to South Africa, my understanding of the boycott as selective, not absolute. I suggested that I might be precisely the kind of person for whom the selectivity of the boycott was intended.

"Did the Prof contact organizations in the democratic movement about his visit?"

This was the one question I did not want to answer. What if one of them was a police spy? What if this university meeting-room was bugged? I pointed out that this was a very sensitive question, especially because I was just now meeting the members of the group for the first time. One of the two white NUSAS students, with whom I had already spent a bit of time and had developed a good relationship, intervened: "Professor Aronson, you can trust everyone here. It's important that you feel free to answer the question openly."

It was difficult, but absolutely necessary. And so I said, simply: "Yes I did."

This was not enough. "What organizations did the Prof contact? Did the Prof contact the forces in exile, such as the ANC?"

I refused to be specific, fearing that it might be my undoing. I certainly could not say that the New York ANC office wanted to speak with me when I got home. Instead, I described my conversation with the visa officer, and then indicated that I had spent several months in discussions with friends, colleagues, and "appropriate people." I talked around it, but finally satisfied them. The questioning went on along a different track: "Will the Prof tell us how he intends to conscientize the masses of South Africa?" They asked about my interests, my contacts, my own organizational affiliations, my purposes. I was struck by the fact that everyone there spoke with respect and self-discipline but without fear of either the professor or potential informers. They were very young, yet probably already veterans of mass uprisings in the townships, remarkably mature and serious in their bearing. And, alas, they already had learned to use the ritualized language of the struggle.

The atmosphere slowly began to thaw, and I realized that I was to be regarded as acceptable when I was asked whether I wanted to meet with people from the democratic movement inside South Africa, and whether I might be willing to talk to these students about American attitudes towards South Africa and the American anti-apartheid movement.

The only sticking point now seemed to involve the procedure by which I was invited: who invited me, and whether student organizations were consulted. This, of course, was a matter internal to the University of Natal, and for a moment it seemed as if my host would himself be placed on the hot seat. Later I found out that a member of the student government (the SRC), an active member of NUSAS, was involved in the decision, and that SANSCO would accept this as consultation. For now, I and the two white students, members of the SRC and NUSAS, were asked to leave while the black students continued by themselves their discussion of the procedures.

I had crossed a major hurdle. Over the next month I was questioned again and again—about the boycott, my invitation, my purposes, the procedures used—and my account was always accepted. Above all it was known that I had been vetted by the SANSCO students, and that was regarded as adequate. Only once in these interactions, in conversation with a prominent white Capetonian who advocated "tightening the noose completely" around South Africa, did I meet any suggestion that I should not have come. It became clear that many people wanted to uphold the principle behind a boycott yet were eager to find a way through the self-defeating effects of making it total. Through a total boycott, as I heard again and again, they would only be cutting themselves off from the people overseas with whom they needed most to interact. As time went on I was told, and came to feel, that my trip was one of the first successful tests of the idea of a *selective* boycott.

I have been describing my process of "coming to" South Africa. Doing so meant developing specific purposes: to interact with South Africans, to develop my thought in relation to the situation, to inject my own learning and perspective into the discussions in the universities—in other words, to practice philosophy there. The next two chapters continue this description of my involvement with South Africa; lecturing there was one of the most gratifying professional experiences of my life, and encountering apartheid was one of the most painful and moving experiences of my life. I tried to give something of myself to the situation in South Africa, and I came to feel deeply for the place and its people.

I think that if I made a contribution it turned out not to be my specific reflections on the Western idea and reality of progress, or the crisis of historical materialism, or Sartre's interaction with Merleau-Ponty over the dialectic. Whatever the specifics of my dozens of statements, I think they were taken as a single, simple message by those, black and white, who so often feel isolated and discouraged: You are not alone. You are part of a larger world. You are part of a world where rational analysis and human values matter, and part of a larger world-historical struggle for social justice. That struggle, inseparable from human reason and its very meaning, goes on in South Africa and elsewhere; those struggling elsewhere look to you in South Africa, just as you look to them. We are your comrades.

However else we may involve ourselves in the struggle in South Africa, it is also necessary to go there and to say this. It is, I think, the essential message any sympathetic intellectual brings to South Africans. And he or she discovers it there as well, perhaps even to carry it home. This message needs to be discovered and presented there dozens of times each year, from one end of the country to the other, in dozens of different ways, in interaction with our South African colleagues and counterparts. It matters a great deal to them.

Part One

Experiencing

I

Lecturing in South Africa

The first time I spoke in public in South Africa reminded me of my first telephone call a year earlier. On the phone from Detroit to Durban, I wanted to talk about the issue of the boycott, so I thought to ask: "Can I speak openly?"

"You'd better not. Overseas calls are known to be monitored," answered the voice from South Africa.

I had grown increasingly comfortable with the man who invited me, and knew I had to find a way to say what was on my mind. It was clumsy enough: "Will I run into any trouble in Harare and Lusaka for coming to Durban?" The main ANC offices are in Zambia, but certain key higher-education people are in Zimbabwe. As I indicated in the introduction, the talk of an ANC boycott had made me very uneasy about accepting the invitation. Crude as my formulation was, he responded without hesitation.

"I don't think you'll have to worry about it at all. The idea of the boycott originated with liberal British academics and the people in Lusaka have gone along with it reluctantly and with many qualifications, and in fact have been somewhat embarrassed by it. You'll find the relevant people here quite receptive."

I asked a few more questions, but my mind was no longer on the boycott. It was rather on the strange new game I was being initiated into: speaking under surveillance. As we talked, I found myself more and more preoccupied with this experience. Certain things could not be said, but had to be talked around, presented in rather transparent code: "Harare" and "Lusaka," "the relevant people." When we said goodbye I sat for a moment, a bit shocked and overwhelmed by the reality.

Preparing to speak publicly in South Africa for the first time a year later, I was told that surveillance was considered part of the routine. Every lecturer at every university expected it, as did every member of every political organization. The tens of thousands of people who have been detained, whether for hours or days or months, bring back with them compelling information about how they've been watched over by the state security police. They are often asked detailed, informed questions about their whereabouts, relationships, and activities, questions based on the work of an elaborate surveillance network.[1] If I was worried about the young comrades from SANSCO disrupting my Hiroshima Day lecture, on "Societal Madness," I was equally worried about how the lecture might sound to the state security police.

I went over the themes with my host to be sure they were not too provocative. I planned to cite instances of societal madness in the twentieth century, to argue that they indeed reflect ruptures with reality, and to explore this phenomenon of rupture more closely. I would end with a question about South Africa: "Are they mad?" But at this stage in my journey I could only ask my audience, not present an answer. Reassured that such thoughts were entirely permissible, and that indeed I had been brought to the university to present them, I went ahead as planned.

The Ubiquity of Politics

"Stay out of politics," I had been told. Looking back on a trip that turned out to be absorbed with politics seven days a week, sixteen hours a day, prompts the question: Did I violate the conditions of my visa? My lectures came to deal more and more with the political reality of South Africa. And in the course of five weeks of intense involvement, my every waking hour came to be pervaded by the same reality. In fact, out of the dozens of discussions I had with my South African colleagues, I can recall only two brief ones—at Stellenbosch and Cape Town—that could have been regarded as normal academic chitchat. Every other discussion, whether I initiated it or not, whether I wanted it or not, was about the situation in South Africa today.

Had I been a businessman, a tourist, or an advisor to the government, I may well have been able to stay away from politics. In fact, neither would I have had to notice apartheid, black poverty, or the pervasiveness of repression. The Royal Hotel in Durban, its luxuries made sweeter by a rand worth less than fifty cents American, is a world away from the University of Natal. An American could happily drift through the "new" South Africa—with its current stress on black education and professional and technical advancement and its absence of humiliating signs—and take no notice that the society remains firmly organized according to racial hierarchy. Which South Africa one sees depends on one's vantage point and one's contacts. And being at the university opened—perhaps imposed—not an ivory-tower image but a view of South Africa that was always political, largely refracted through the lenses of its opposition.

In fact, most of the people I met were political, ranging from the president of the University of Durban-Westville Students Representative Council who had just been released from 113 days of detention; to a dissident Afrikaner academic who had been part of the Dakar delegation to meet the ANC; to one of the few national United Democratic Front leaders not in detention; to a fierce supporter of the government who took me on a whirlwind trip to the Durban market; to a man who had served five and a half years in a Transkei prison and whose step-brother had been murdered by the Transkei police two years ago (and who was himself detained for protesting the murder).

In addition I visited African townships, Indian and "colored" group-areas, white residential and commercial areas, the port and Indian market of Durban, Bophuthatswana, the Cape peninsula, the "gray areas" of Johannesburg (the market, city center on Saturday, Joubert Park and Hillbrow) where whites and blacks mingle freely and even live side by side in violation of the Group Areas Act. And among the many people I spent time with were Afrikaner students who had refused military service, English- and Afrikaans-speaking supporters of government policy, activists in the Detainees' Parents Support Committee, and students who had met with the ANC.

The most social of conversations at parties would begin with: "How do you like South Africa?" Sometimes the question was more challenging ("Is it better or worse than the propaganda in the American media?") or even more provocative ("Will you go home and write bad things about us?"). Americans are few and far between, American academics fewer, and American academics with some "political" interest are veritable lightning rods.

Even usually apolitical people insisted on talking politics. The departmental secretary, a middle-class white woman, feeling concerned about my hectic schedule and my constant political involvement, invited a colleague and me to dinner with her and her husband at their lovely country home. This planned respite from politics itself was overshadowed by the inevitable question, What is going to happen in South Africa? At the end of a highly charged evening of conversation about Afrikaners, emigration, the UDF, and the ANC, our hostess apologized, to general laughter, for another session of politics.

Speaking in a Revolutionary Situation

The reason for the obsession is simple enough: South Africa is in the midst of what can only be called a constitutional or even a revolutionary crisis. At stake is what the future South Africa will look like and who will have the power to shape it. The state has constitutionally defined itself as representing only a small minority of South Africans but is stamped as illegitimate by the rest. Because the vast majority has begun to act against it, the minority Nationalist government rules by emergency decree, controlling information, restricting organizations from any political activity, banning meetings, keeping the opposition off-balance by detention (over thirty thousand people have been detained since the beginning of the state of emergency in July 1985, most of them connected with the UDF), and by even worse measures. But as everyone knows, brute force cannot create a consensus which is prohibited on principle. The government's continued effort to rebottle apartheid's old wine only highlights, but can never resolve, the constitutional crisis. Daily life in such an intrinsically revolutionary situation, however normal it may otherwise seem, cannot help but be dominated by politics, though for affluent white professionals this may take the guise of learning each day that someone else has decided to emigrate.

Even at a university such as Natal, whose subtropical surroundings remind one of UCLA (and whose surrounding residences recall Los Angeles' Westwood Village), the most apolitical male student will be asking whether to stay or leave after graduation, when military service beckons. I was told that 6 percent of Durban's affluent Jewish community had left in the previous eighteen months; that one-third of the medical students who had graduated from the University of the Witwatersrand in Johannesburg during the previous four years had already emigrated; and that another one-third were contemplating or planning emigration.

As I lectured, the revolutionary character of the situation came home to me rather unexpectedly. Before my first lecture I worried about how people in South Africa would respond. After all, what importance could the reflections of an American philosopher, developed half a world away, have for people living in a situation with such pressing urgencies? Yet as I spoke about societal madness in the twentieth century I sensed an alertness in the audience that I hadn't felt even in the late 1960s in the United States. My other lectures—about the repressive side of progress, for example, or responsibility for and complicity with evil, or the world-historical struggle for human dignity—met with equally strong interest. As time went on, I realized that the more I gave, the greater was the response, until I found myself more fully involved, more completely practicing philosophy, than ever before in my life.

Whenever I spoke, I had a simple but remarkable experience. People were engaged directly, they listened carefully and asked thoughtful, even searching questions. The ideas were not taken as being "just" ideas, dismissed because they had nothing to do with immediate issues and concerns; nor were they taken as ideology, to be fought against or defended insofar as they corresponded to the listener's own body of beliefs. Instead, the ideas were discussed seriously as possible ways of comprehending the situation people found themselves in, as potential lenses that could be tried on and used. For example, each time I gave a lecture on the crisis of historical materialism, in four different settings, I was met by a vigorous response leading to the most energetic debate. For all their alleged obsolescence in the West, in South Africa I found that Marxian ideas are taken totally seriously—not as doctrine, but as potential ways of explaining experience. A lecturer can tell this by reading the many and various, often subliminal, nuances of audience response, as well as by noticing what questions are asked and how they are phrased. After giving dozens of lectures I concluded that at this moment in history, ideas are far more alive in South Africa than in the United States.

Of course one should avoid romanticizing the situation. Many colleagues complained about the anti-intellectualism of many of the politically most active students, their aversion for the hard mental effort of thinking through questions, exploring premises, and constructing rational arguments about their deeply held beliefs. Once the political issues surrounding my visit were resolved, the SANSCO students never responded to my efforts to meet them again and discuss a topic of their choosing. Colleagues complained that activists are often theoretically very dogmatic and simplistic and see no reason to be otherwise. Boycotts are declared by small groups and violently imposed on others, who are beat up if they refuse to go along: no discussion or choice. Certainly the situation is grim in many ways, and the grimness is mirrored in the practices of the movement.

Still, from any conversation in such a situation, it becomes clear that radical change—whether it is seen as inevitable or doubtful, as a threat, an uncertainty, a promise, or a mixed blessing—is very much on everyone's mind. This fact imparts a special tone of openness towards the future, a sense of change being in the air, in question after question. In this climate, to "stay out of politics" was truly impossible. To avoid politics in South Africa today would be to miss South Africa.

Walking on Eggshells

Inevitably, then, my university lectures began to explore parallels between South Africa and other historical situations I had studied. Even so, I never made the kind of pronouncements—denunciations of apartheid or statements in support of the ANC—that so worried the visa officer. Nor did I engage in the kind of politics I suspect she had in mind: I never became directly involved in a demonstration or something that might be considered a political activity; I carried no messages for particular individuals in or out of the country. In these senses I did indeed "stay out of politics."

Nevertheless, even if my interventions were analytical and based on research and reflection, never straying from the topic at hand, her warning was effective. It alerted me that South Africa was not the United States, that being there was serious business, and that whatever I did or did not do—indeed, whatever I said—would have consequences. It kept me apprehensive at each lecture I gave, each statement I made; I knew that I walked the narrow line of what was permitted to a foreign visitor, and I constantly wondered if I was about to cross that line.

Was it too far-fetched to think, in a country where between 1,500 (government figure) and 5,000 (Detainees' Parents Support Committee estimate) people were currently being detained, that an American lecturer might hear a knock on the door in the middle of the night that would lead to his expulsion? Each day I pushed the line a bit further, wondering whether informers would report something that would ring a bell in the state security police office. The process continued that I had initiated from afar in my first phone call and begun in person in my first public lecture. I learned how to speak as I never had to before, even—or especially—in the 1960s: elliptically, suggestively, attributing my most provocative opinions to "Americans" or posing them hypothetically. In short, I learned how to behave as the vast majority of South Africans do in order to survive.

It was an unaccustomed experience of walking on eggshells, of learning the limits of what I might be able to say, and slowly, daily, stretching those limits. But was a police agent really listening? It felt a bit like jousting with windmills, facing an invisible opponent who, in fact, might not be there at all. And if I stepped over the unseen limits, what would happen? How much attention would the state really pay to an anonymous American academic?

Over the weeks, as I built up a dense network of contacts and was asked to give more and more talks, some of them off-campus, my self-confidence grew. It began to dawn on me that even in the unlikely event that my visit was actually raising eyebrows in the state security service, expelling me would create a scandal, and the accompanying publicity would defeat any possible purpose of the expulsion. In other words, the support I received from my audiences seemed to protect me against an interruption of my trip. If I had indeed crossed an invisible line, it seemed more and more likely that I wouldn't know until and unless I applied for a visa to return.

And so I made use of the privilege of being an outsider. In the proper context and with careful preparation I could, after all, speak about the week-long series on the ANC in the *Detroit Free Press* that previous April, about Oliver Tambo's appearance on Canadian television, or about American attitudes towards apartheid, or even about sanctions. Everyone wanted to know whether Ronald Reagan's and Jesse Helm's pro-apartheid sympathies, as depicted by the South African Broadcasting Corporation (SABC), reflected the American mainstream. Questions like these were asked at off-campus talks, such as the one I gave to the National Medical and Dental Association (NAMDA). Each time these issues came up, the room hushed until one could hear a pin drop; it was as if we had entered forbidden yet sacred ground.

Themes and Audiences

I had been scheduled to give a total of nineteen lectures at the University of Natal, three sets of five, to first-, second-, and third-year political science students, as well as two public lectures and two staff seminars. To the more than one hundred first-year students, of whom about fifteen were black, I developed at length the theme of my Hiroshima Day lecture, "The Dialectics of Disaster": the irrational politics of the twentieth century and their catastrophic results. I concluded the final first-year lecture with the same question that I used in the public lecture: To what extent has South Africa been bitten by the same kind of irrationality that gripped Nazi Germany? Or, to put it another way, if and when pushed far enough, will key elements in white South Africa cut a deal? This was one of the main questions I had brought with me into the country, and it became one of the main themes of hours of discussion. Every time I discussed the Holocaust or Stalinism, this question was posed about South Africa (see chapter 5 below).

I assigned Turgot, Condorcet, and Comte to the twenty-odd second-year students, about five of whom were black, and lectured to them about "The Fetishization of Progress." I attempted to show how the idea of progress that was developed by Condorcet subsequently became purged of its critical social and political dimensions, its democracy and equality, and was fetishized by Comte into efficiency and technological progress. And I applied this analysis, too, to the time and place. After my introduction, a student (I later found out he was an activist with NUSAS, the student organization) raised his hand and stated that the current debate in South Africa was precisely over what form progress was to take. Would it involve technological improvements only and leave social and political arrangements largely in place, or would its goal be progress towards democracy and equality? Both the black and white students who spoke were skeptical about whether the project of economic progress without political equality could succeed;

a black student identified such progress as the goal of Anglo-American Corporation, the giant that dominates the South African economy (as formulated by its chief scenario planner, Clem Sunter in *The World and South Africa in the 1990s*).[2] And so the students lent a special charge to the remaining sessions, which were devoted to exploring the roots, developments, and contradictions of the Enlightenment idea. Along the way, in reading Condorcet, we noticed the remarkable fact that his justification for colonialism was bound up with his notion of reason and progress. His belief in progress, and in France's political and social accomplishments, dictated his seeing the non-Western world as backward and in need of Western-style progress. Condorcet was no racist; he simply believed that Europe was more advanced and had the right and obligation to impose its social forms on the rest of the world. The most powerful moment of these sessions was the one in which it became clear that one of the most liberating themes of Western thought, Condorcet's Enlightenment concept of reason, went hand in hand with the West's domination of the non-Western world.

With the dozen third-year students, of whom only one or two were black, I had a series of discussions on politics in the United States, beginning with their questions and focusing on American ideas about, and experiences of, freedom. They were particularly interested in what was generally regarded in South Africa as the "hypocritical" American attitude toward apartheid. The SABC, the highly ideological government television network, had shown "Eyes on the Prize," the documentary about the civil rights movement—certainly not to stimulate black struggle in South Africa but more likely in order to demonstrate the viciousness, strength, and persistence of American racism. How, the students asked, could such a society—indeed, a capitalist and imperialist society—presume to judge South African racism? The more conservative *and* the more radical students seemed to agree on our hypocrisy, and both groups stressed our many unresolved problems and worldwide imperial role. Teaching in a program half of whose student are black adults, at Detroit's Wayne State University, I had learned my answer well before leaving for South Africa. In discussions where the "danger of Communism" had been posed, I had been told that, even if Communism should somehow take over in South Africa, and even if it is as bad as claimed, it is still better than apartheid. No form of oppression is as painful, as humiliating, as brutal, as backward, as having your life determined by the color of your skin—that is, by something you are born with, something totally beyond your control. Nothing can be worse than a social system that legislates this kind of oppression and openly organizes itself according to it.

This answer, gift of American blacks to South African conservatives, liberals, and radicals, silenced all resistance in a very resistant group. It stressed that South Africa is regarded as the moral leper of the world for very good reason. With all their many problems, other countries have at least freed themselves from statutory racial hierarchy, that most repulsive heritage of the four-hundred-year-old white Western domination of people of color. In this sense South Africa has the most backward social relations in the world today.

As time went on more invitations came. I was invited to lead a seminar at the University of Durban-Westville, most of whose students are Indian. I was asked to give a sermon to a Jewish congregation, lectures to classes in German literature and psychology, and a keynote address to the Durban regional branch of NAMDA (the National Medical and Dental Association). Arrangements were made for me to spend a week at the predominantly "colored" University of the Western Cape, as well as lectures and seminars at the Universities of Cape Town and Stellenbosch. In addition, I gave a talk to the only Afrikaner chapter of NUSAS, at Stellenbosch, and presented an English department seminar on "Intellectuals and Politics" at Cape Town. Finally, on my way out of South Africa, I spoke in Johannesburg on the Israeli-Palestinian conflict, first to a meeting of Habonim, a Zionist youth group, and later to the leadership of Jews for Social Justice, an anti-apartheid organization.

Each of these occasions had its own special features. Speaking to NUSAS at Natal, for example, was totally different from speaking to NUSAS at Stellenbosch. Before the first session I had already gotten to know many of the students in Durban and was respected and trusted by them. Many of them had come to my lectures, and several of us had dinner together the week before at a student commune. In a late-afternoon session of questions and answers I now told them that I thought that their tensions and perplexities were inevitable, since they were white students seeking to bring about black majority rule. I stressed what I saw as the main issue for them, namely, keeping their commitment alive in an extremely difficult situation, one that was bound to get more difficult.

I thought that some lessons from America during the 1960s might be useful in South Africa during the 1980s. White activists have an enormously complex role in a movement for black liberation. At this moment in South African history, both the state and the democratic movement see the students as being of great importance. The state detains and harasses them, and the UDF encourages and supports them. Because they work in one of the few relatively free spaces remaining in South Africa, their activism has survived the repression. Not only do they keep alive the sense of movement at a crucial time, but they contribute to a main strategic direction for the democratic movement's political activity: to gain significant support among English-speaking and Afrikaans-speaking whites.

Guilt politics is unavoidable but dangerous, especially when provocateurs try to push the guilty into violence.[3] Recalling ideas developed during the 1960s, I emphasized that, even if students are driven by guilt about their privileged status and by a commitment to equality, they can make an important contribution in the long run by placing themselves at the center of their politics. In supporting the black movement, they are also rebelling *for themselves* against the oppressiveness of being oppressors. Their own liberation as white Africans depends on the transformation of South Africa. For their own sake, and the movement's, they must learn to see their commitment for what it is—a courageous and noble one, motivated by shame, love, and hope—and to appreciate it as such. At the very least, it will keep them from being overwhelmed by the dreadful facts of black oppression and state repression, by the enormity of their own tasks and their human weaknesses.

This discussion, which took place on the last Friday I was at Natal, was for me a high point of four weeks of interaction with young people I had come to respect and love. Five days later, I carried these feelings with me into a meeting with Stellenbosch NUSAS. But now I was a stranger speaking to Afrikaners, who were more deferential, in the old town of Stellenbosch. Set in the heart of the wine country, Stellenbosch resembles Palo Alto in its upper-middle-class stateliness. The University of Stellenbosch has educated every Afrikaner head of government before P. W. Botha; its buildings and surroundings date to the earliest days of Dutch settlement and are suggestive of both Oxford and Cambridge. Intellectually, both students and faculty were unusual as well; nowhere in all of South Africa was there greater interest in and knowledge of Sartre's works. The seminar I led there was challenging and exciting.

My evening session with Stellenbosch NUSAS began with my impressions of South Africa. I was surprised, I said, by the extent of state political repression on the one hand and of black poverty on the other. But neither had I anticipated the extent, depth, or high morale of the democratic movement, even under repression. I spoke briefly and asked for questions. As if to explain the embarrassing moment of silence, the student closest to me said: "You're still a Prof." Of course that was one inhibiting factor; the other was that I was an anti-apartheid American talking to Afrikaners.

I had prepared for this session by thinking about the predicament of Afrikaner dissidents. I discussed the issue with a number of people, among them an Afrikaner psychologist whose dissertation had studied the older generation. She had stressed the extent to which the Afrikaner identity has come to be bound up with a project and its ideology—racial domination—and is so tightly organized as to leave little space to declare oneself a different kind of Afrikaner, one committed to equality and social justice. Thus dissidents refer to themselves as "Afrikaans-speaking"; they align themselves with English-speakers or feel themselves as outsiders, rather than forming into groups laying claim to the identity itself. Several people contrasted the ease with which young English South Africans move from one political position to another with the slow, careful, and ultimately profound political conversions undergone by Afrikaners who become anti-racists. An entire cultural orientation is not jettisoned so casually; bridges to one's community are not burned so lightly.[4]

In the same way, Afrikaner student activists, unlike their English-speaking counterparts, generally refuse to accept a political line without considerable reflection; unwilling to be dominated by expedience, they explore a full range of alternatives. Is there a prospect for an anti-apartheid Afrikaner movement to emerge *within* the community? I asked this in talking to the Stellenbosch students, collectively and individually, and later with other dissident Afrikaners. In one discussion a few of us imagined how a group of Afrikaners committed against apartheid might gather to explore common ground and ways of attracting others of like mind. The project would involve reappropriating cultural symbols, rethinking the past, and shaping a new unity in which old values could be joined to ideas of universal justice.

This would, above all, be a new creation, but it seems that many dissidents are repulsed by the idea of squandering their time on the community from which they have been trying to free themselves, especially given the opprobrium they have had to bear. Still, mindful of how difficult it has often been for American Jews to swim against the current and criticize Israel, I pressed the issue. Those who worry hysterically about Afrikaner survival under majority rule, and so justify continuing apartheid, perhaps to the point of accepting Armageddon, need to be answered. And in a twofold way: by rethinking Afrikaner identity so that it can become compatible with the equality of other identities; and by stressing that long-term self-interest depends on the most rapid possible accommodation. The dissidents can offer a better way to preserve the community: by negotiating a solution while negotiation between equals is still possible, before hatred and polarization make negotiation unthinkable. Although this is not a popular position, such arguments can best be developed by Afrikaners talking to other Afrikaners.

Lessons from Jewish experience figured in some other talks I gave, but also in one I did *not* give—a sermon at a Durban synagogue on "Lessons of the Holocaust for South African Jews." After agreeing to this topic, the rabbi phoned early the next day and said that, upon reflection, it might be better for me to speak about "Getting beyond Mutual Denial in the Israeli-Palestinian Conflict." Was the original theme too controversial? (This would mean that I had done the impossible—discovered an even more controversial issue than the Israeli-Palestinian conflict!) But the rabbi assured me that he had concluded that this topic would be "more interesting," and I acceded.

The night before, I had witnessed a community meeting that might explain any possible sensitivity about delving too far into the question of how to respond to apartheid. There I learned of the threefold response of the official Jewish community to the current situation in South Africa: a principled position against apartheid, supplemented by pronouncements against current state actions; generous support of charitable, educational, and self-help programs for the black community; and a concerted effort to keep Israel from imposing sanctions. On this last point Jewish anti-apartheid groups, such as Jews for Social Justice in Johannesburg, dissent, arguing that the third action is the one that really counts, because it is the community's only explicitly political act and it expresses a practical complicity with the apartheid state by keeping Israeli weapons flowing. In fact, as recent election results show, South Africa's 120,000 Jews are evenly split on apartheid. As the leader of Durban's Jewish community told me, without betraying so much as a hint of approbation or disapprobation, there were now two Nationalist as well as two Progressive Federal members of parliament who were Jews.

When I presented my Holocaust talk in the slightly different guise of an academic lecture, I learned just how controversial it might be to both Jews and non-Jews. Lecturing to a German class at Natal and, later, before a political ethics class at the University of Cape Town, I asked: Who was responsible for murdering six million Jews? I argued that the spiral of responsibility moved from those who ordered, planned, and directly carried out the "Final Solution to the Jewish Problem," to all those who staffed the apparatus, to the Nazi party members, to another ten million Germans who voted to put the Nazis in power in the last free elections, in 1932, to the millions of "good Germans" who paid their taxes and later lamented Hitler's policies and/or claimed ignorance of what was going on, to powerful groups outside of Germany— government officials, members of the political elites, and even some Jewish political leaders—who allowed it to happen.

My main point was to focus on those who allow evil to happen in their name, whose taxes and military service and acquiescence keep their governments functioning, and who therefore must be described as complicit. I suggested parallels with all those white English-speaking South Africans I had met who professed hostility to apartheid and even to Afrikaner political domination, but still accepted them. (This lecture appears below as chapter 3.)

This was the first lecture in which normally polite South African students—and they are even more polite at Cape Town—interrupted before I could finish. In Durban I was accused of "attacking the entire German people." In Cape Town an older man defended the Jewish leadership in the United States: "What else could they have done?" Younger people couldn't understand how I could be suggesting that any state action—or indeed any action—could be described as evil. "What basis do you have for morally judging any action?"

So far I have been describing interactions with largely white groups. Largely black ("colored", African, and/or Indian) audiences and student groups were always less restrained and more unanimously politically aligned. Their questions were provocative at a different level: they clearly saw themselves as partisans in the current situation, and they were more directly looking for usable tools and insights. At Durban-Westville I was asked to comment on the UDF strategy of remaining parallel to, but separate from, the trade union movement, the Congress of South African Trade Unions (COSATU); before the National Medical and Dental Association (NAMDA) I was asked to discuss the issue of American sanctions. One of the most stimulating discussions took place in a philosophy of science class at the University of the Western Cape. On the previous day at this highly politicized campus there had been a student strike in response to the execution of two young ANC members for allegedly killing a township official and his family during the explosion of 1984. As a police helicopter buzzed menacingly overhead, more than two thousand students rallied to protest the execution. At 8:45 the next morning no one was sure whether the students thought classes were on or off.

A different kind of chaos was also evident on campus. The university has expanded so much and so quickly that sessions had been reduced to thirty-five minutes, and even finding classrooms had become a major problem. Construction was everywhere. The class I taught was held in a temporary building next to the site of the excavation for a new administration building, and the noise of the work filled the room.

Given the political temperature of the previous day, I decided to begin with a class discussion, based on a four-page insert in that day's *Cape Times*, about the newly completed Du Toit's Kloof tunnel, which saves eleven kilometers of mountain travel by speeding traffic through four kilometers of mountain at a cost of 145 million rand (75 million dollars), projected to be recovered in twenty years. "Is this progress?" I asked. After looking over the supplement, the students, all of whom knew about the tunnel, reflexively agreed: it would help save time and, eventually, money. The discussion soon shifted to who controls progress, and who benefits from it; it quickened as one student laid out the terms of real progress "for the people" that would include not only the obvious food, shelter, and education but also weapons. Weapons? Was this young "colored" man promoting the progress of the South African Defense Forces? Upon questioning, it became clear what he meant. Real progress meant increasing the people's ability to defend themselves against the state, and therefore weapons for the townships were necessary. No one disagreed, although one or two preferred changing the state so as not to have to defend oneself against it.

As so often happens in a good class, the discussion was upset and then redefined by a student, in this case one who attacked the "Western notion" of scientific and technological progress. Another responded to him, arguing that the Western notion was the only one they had, and that its key terms were beneficial. The confrontation between them was especially charged, and went on for several minutes. It obviously focused a central question for people throughout the Third World: To what extent are they fatally caught in the Western project, condemned to find their way through it using Western tools and concepts; or are there meaningful alternatives to Western-style development and industrialization? Even though they are still suffering from the way the West imposed itself on them, could they use the West to liberate themselves?

This was no abstract discussion among people pondering someone else's problems. As "coloreds" and Africans studying philosophy in order to grasp their own reality, they could not distinguish their personal ambitions from the transformation they anticipate for South Africa—or from the sounds of conflict. The noise outside was from construction that benefited them; the police helicopter hovering overhead yesterday during the rally represented the enemy. Even in this time of repression, politics was in the air everywhere. The constitutional crisis cannot be detained. No wonder lecturing in South Africa was so deeply satisfying—because the atmosphere is alive with change, because ideas matter to people, because people are looking for ways of thinking about a reality that is in crisis. In short, because what one says has consequences.

Danger

Sometimes the consequences are unexpected. I have said that I became more confident as the weeks went by. Perhaps too confident—so I was to learn in Cape Town. Nothing scandalous happened during my many lectures. My major public lecture at Natal (presented below as chapter 4) was followed by an interview with a reporter for the *Natal Daily News*. A colleague sat with me during the interview, and he read the article before it was submitted to make sure nothing politically compromising had inadvertently found its way in. But it was still a relief to learn that I would be safely out of the country before the article was to be published (in the end, it never appeared). Nevertheless, I remained somewhat anxious. After my wife returned to the United States, I worried as I went to bed alone each night in the visitor's flat in the university's main classroom building. Perhaps I had spoken too much with people who had been detained, had become frightened by their description of the knock on the door in the middle of the night. In any case, during my final week I was happy to be staying with a colleague at his flat in Cape Town, finding that I slept more securely in someone's home.

Until the middle of the week. Wednesday night, before turning in, I went to get my journal so I could reflect on the day. Keeping the journal had become a ritual of my trip, and it included comments on my reading before I left for South Africa, detailed reflections on meetings and discussions, accounts of conversations, descriptions of places I had seen, notes and ideas for possible writings on my trip, outlines for lectures, and detailed analyses of the political situation. That almost full two-hundred-page black book with a bright floral cover had become, by this point, a precious possession. Even before entering South Africa I had worried enough about the customs inspection to omit key words wherever I mentioned something the state security service might find sensitive, and I continued this practice while in the country. I worried about the journal enough to remember, after writing in it, exactly where I left it, and normally did not take it out with me during the day.

This evening, however, it was not where I had left it, at the end of the dining table next to a window overlooking Table Mountain. So I went to the bedroom where it surely would be. Not there either. Nor in my shoulder bag. Now my friend and I both began to worry, and started looking seriously, turning the flat upside down. It was nowhere to be found. We carefully reviewed where I had been that day and decided to phone everyone and everywhere the next morning. I went to bed, hoping I had done the unthinkable, namely, taken it out of the flat, and that it would turn up at my office at the University of the Western Cape or at the colleague's office I had used at the University of Cape Town or in the car that had taken me from the one to the other. By noon the next day all the necessary phone calls had been made, and the journal had not turned up. It was clearly missing. But how could I have lost it? I was sitting with my host and a friend, and as my mind kept thinking back to the last place I saw it I reflexively kept reaching back across to the end of the table.

And then it dawned on us: perhaps the state security police had entered the flat and removed the notebook. This was at least as possible as anything else. Instead of blaming myself for forgetfulness, I had to face the fact that the notebook might have been taken, and turn to the possible implications. And so with my host and the friend—himself a veteran of several detentions and several years in prison—I began to think my way through what might happen. Could the journal itself endanger anyone? While I avoided mentioning names in it, often leaving blanks, in one case I named a person in hiding whom I had met. I also presented a detailed analysis of current UDF strategy. Neither this, nor anything else I had written about, would be important, but perhaps it might incite the security apparatus to take an interest in this American, to see what else he knew or who else he had contacted in South Africa or overseas. Would I be picked up for questioning? Would I be detained before departure?

The questions before me were the same questions tens of thousands of South Africans have faced in the recent past. What is the likelihood of being detained? What would the state be after? How long would they hold me? How would they treat me? How should I respond? I was fortunate to be able to discuss this in detail with experienced people, who could help me convert my state of helpless outrage to one of active preparation. The likelihood of my being stopped, we agreed, was not great, if for no other reason than that I was harmless: I was a visiting lecturer, with no organizational connections or mission, and at this moment the security police had far more important fish to fry. Vigilantes and political repression have become normal in South Africa, but they are tied to active efforts to organize opposition. Still, something that I had said at a lecture, and its elaboration in my journal, might have caught someone's eye. Tuesday night at Stellenbosch, for example, I had been unusually open about the ANC. Immediately afterwards I worried about having said too much. So it was best to be prepared, even against unlikely possibilities.

I might be stopped at any time between now and my departure later in the week, even if just for brief questioning. How efficient was the security service? My name was in the South African Airways computer as traveling to Johannesburg on Friday and to Frankfurt on Saturday. It would be easy enough to track me down. If questioned, I was advised, I should tell the truth whenever pressed, as long as it didn't implicate anyone else, but above all I should insist on the academic nature of my visit. And my friends and I set about alerting people about the possibility of my being detained, so that if I was, my congressman's offices in Detroit and Washington could immediately contact the American consulate in Johannesburg. A number of discussions, a number of phone calls, and I was as prepared as I was going to be. I would be relieved, I joked several times, to be stopped, for then I would know who had my journal, and would be able to ask for it back. But this was bravado. I slept fitfully, expecting (whether realistically or not) the decisive moments to be those when I would board the plane from Cape Town to Johannesburg and, on the following day, when I would leave Johannesburg—and South Africa—for Frankfurt. Friends would wait with me until I cleared the check-in counter in the first instance and customs in the second, and then they would make telephone calls to other friends. My friends always believed it was unlikely I would be stopped. In a state of emergency, however, one learns to live by taking precautions. The anxiety may recede but it never goes away. And it is worse for, say, an American who is unaccustomed to such conditions. I fully expected someone to stop me at check-in at Cape Town or at passport control in Johannesburg; I would be questioned and then, I hoped, allowed to board my plane.

As it turned out, nothing happened. At Cape Town several friends brought me to the check-in counter. They all waited with me until boarding time. The next day in Johannesburg I was accompanied by two friends. I checked in, was assigned my seat, and then, after tentative good-byes, I cleared baggage search and passport control. My friends had been waiting on the other side of the glass, and once they saw I was clear, we all waved.

One month later, safely home in Detroit, I received a letter from my host in Cape Town. Two weeks after I left, a Stellenbosch student who had heard me speak to NUSAS brought my journal to him. My friend was a bit puzzled about why it had taken so long, but in any event he sent it out immediately by registered mail. The package arrived three months later, with one of the seals broken. Perhaps I really did unthinkingly leave my journal at Stellenbosch, after all, and perhaps my visit went entirely unnoticed. Perhaps not. Perhaps the journal was taken, and read, and returned. I may never know; I may find out if and when I apply for a new visa; or I may hear about it sometime during my next visit. But it doesn't really matter. There are people who are suffering far more than I, a privileged foreign visitor who, when my momentary anxiety was over, could go back home and resume normal life. The incident gave me a taste, only a taste, of the daily life of my counterparts in South Africa.

My last moment in South Africa, protected by friends, recalled my first moments in the South African Airways queue at Heathrow Airport five weeks earlier. After a few words of introduction, an Indian physician who was returning from a medical conference in London immediately befriended my wife and me. He waited for us, guided us onto the plane, and came over to our seats for an intense late-night conversation with my wife about what it was like to be black in South Africa. Of course he was glad to be going home to his family, but at the same time he was pained to be heading back to second-class citizenship, to his group area, to a black hospital where patients lay on floors waiting for a bed. Upon our arrival in Durban he waited and again guided us through customs. I saw him several times again, and we became good friends. I learned only later that he was a political activist.

As I have said, my last images of South Africa are also of friends: friends at Cape Town sitting with me until boarding was announced; friends in Johannesburg following me around the glassed-in area at Jan Smuts Airport, watching as I cleared inspection, then watching as I cleared passport control. I didn't stop for our final wave, but I was enormously relieved. They would phone the friends in Cape Town to tell them everything was all right. How many times had people like these made similar phone calls? In London, Durban, Cape Town, and Johannesburg, I had been taken care of by both blacks and whites. The doctor had watched over us as we were coming in; now I was being watched over as I was leaving. Strange, but these remain my fondest images of lecturing in South Africa—moving gestures, from people who themselves need watching over.

2

Terrible Simplicity

Before going to South Africa I often wondered whether the evil of apartheid is something that screams out at you, embarrassing and outrageous, or whether it is just another nasty form of daily life. Once there, I first found it to be a bit of both, and often bewilderingly: routines and patterns seemingly accepted by everyone, scarcely worthy of notice, suddenly gave way in my perception to the bizarre and shocking. The normal appearance of everyday life suddenly vanishes before some brutal twist of contemporary social engineering, or a startling note of Western arrogance, or a blatantly asserted inequality, and you feel yourself to be in another world. While having lunch downtown on a bright winter's day, someone tells you about their time spent in detention, shows you the building in the center of Durban where they were held, and describes the interrogating methods used by the bureau of state security.

Or you are hurried out of a staff seminar to be taken to visit a prominent UDF leader in hiding, and find yourself driving, walking, then driving and walking again to get to the person without being followed. Or, shopping for groceries, you notice as you leave that the black person who was in the shop when you walked in had been made to wait to be served until after you. Or, going over your lecture notes for the next class, you look out of the window and see a police helicopter hovering menacingly over a student demonstration. Or, visiting a township, you notice the fortified single entrance waiting to be sealed off in the case of "unrest." Or, going to have dinner and an evening of conversation, you notice little knots of black people, servants on their time off, hanging out together on street corners and in a park in a white group-area.

Can this be normal? And then, before you can even think about rights and wrongs, the last image disappears and you are at dinner, being offered wonderful curries and excellent wines. And then, after one such lively evening with Indian and African professionals, the Africans begin gathering themselves for their drive back to their four-room township homes. Instantly, a dignified, sophisticated medical professor with a delightful sense of humor gets ready to become a "kaffir" again, and an Indian friend remarks, bitterly, that "it's return to your group-areas time."

The outsider will observe apartheid through dozens of such moments of daily life, totally normal yet undeniably painful. Which is to say that, like any social reality, South Africa's is complex and ambiguous. As in any society, even the most brutal oppression appears within and through normal patterns of daily life in which people even try to pursue their well-being as humanely and cooperatively as possible.

How then is one to make one's way through the kaleidoscopic and even contradictory perceptions of South Africa? Which among thousands of impressions does one select as best expressing the place? I found myself experiencing the appalling simplicity within the complexity, and then, later, reflecting on some of the ambiguities that abound within such apparent clarity. This book will follow the same path. In this chapter I will return to the beginning of my trip and tell the story of this visitor's experience of apartheid. Then, in chapters 5 and 6, after presenting two of my professional responses to South Africa in chapters 3 and 4, I will explore some of the complexities of the current situation and their roots. The descriptions that follow suggest that, at the moral and political core of all of its intricacies, apartheid has a terrible simplicity to it. They will explain why the weeks of my stay were a time of full involvement in a situation where everything came to seem particularly clear, urgent, and filled with meaning.

Apartheid in Gold Class

It seemed a premonition of racial privilege to be bumped to gold class on our South African Airways flight from London to Durban while our new physician friend, an Indian, somehow missed the bump and stayed in economy class. We were granted a taste of an all-white world of affluence—being asked by our white stewards to choose from ten wines during the course of the dinner, being offered brandies and liqueurs (which I brought back to our less fortunate patron, who in turn gave them to those sitting around him). Our arrival in the extra-large seats seemed to announce equally arbitrary processes in which one had to do nothing other than be white to be endowed with special claims to well-being.

But, after such a beginning "in" South Africa, I was puzzled by the musical offering on the airplane's channel 2: "Spotlight on Paul Simon." In the United States the Graceland tour, featuring Ladysmith Black Mambazo, Hugh Masakela, and Miriam Makeba, along with Simon, had been received as an anti-apartheid event, concluding with rousing versions of "Nkosi Sikale'l l'Africa." Anti-apartheid activist David Webster was later to play the Graceland album for me with great pleasure. But how could Simon, in jeans, decorate the cover of the South African Airways program that announced a one-hour taped interview with fifteen songs? How could the anti-apartheid "Graceland" become acceptable, indeed useful, enough for the government airways to include it?

Indeed, did this mean that our white pilots were flying us towards one of those ambiguous, confusing places of the world that required analysis, reflection, clarification at every step in order to avoid muddle? The Simon tape was smoothly hosted by an American, one Bob Taylor, and even allowed Ladysmith Black Mambazo two songs and contained what Simon described as a protest song, "Homeless." Simon's encounter with Africa was presented as that of the white entrepreneur/music expert who discovered the unlettered diamond-in-the-rough blacks and, after assembling and polishing them, brought them into the outside world. In short, the message (whatever Simon himself might have intended by the interview) seemed tailor-made for the South African state: on the surface, tolerance of a broad range of opinion, even including anti-apartheid sentiments; beneath the surface, whites leading blacks, educating them, bringing them the benefits of white civilization and know-how (after all, some of them couldn't read music, Simon said).

Obviously, Simon had no understanding of what he had let himself in for. In this interview he was being shamelessly manipulated, and he unwittingly served apartheid, even as the liberal-appearing South African Airways let him protest about African homelessness. Beneath his generosity appeared a positively colonial message. Thus Simon could appear pro-black and anti-black at the same time, much the way any apologist for apartheid appears.

By the end of the second day in Durban my wife and I were still wrestling with our perceptions. Durban was impressively modern and new, its downtown landscape infinitely better-off than, say, downtown Detroit. And there were no visible tokens of apartheid. In fact only twice in five weeks did we see "whites only" or "blacks only" signs—at Beachfront in Durban and at a black cemetery in the Natal Midlands. Indeed, I rode in buses with blacks, went to integrated jazz clubs, and later entered a predominantly white restaurant in Seapoint, Cape Town, with a black friend and was served without hesitation. On this second night dinner was at an excellent offbeat Italian restaurant with a cute Chicago gangster theme, La Mafia. The kitchen staff and a second-level waitress were black (unusual in American Italian restaurants), but aside from that we could have been back home. After dinner we found ourselves to be the only pedestrians walking through a somewhat sinister area of automobile showrooms to the center of downtown, where, as recommended, we entered the five-star Royal Hotel for coffee. We could have been in the coffee shop of Detroit's Michigan Inn or Westin Hotel. Seated just behind us was a middle-class black couple, finishing a late dinner.

Searching for apartheid, we realized that we were, unexpectedly, enjoying ourselves! Where, then, was the most brutal and inhumane social system of the world today? We knew it lay out there, beyond us, in some sense underneath us, but we had not seen it yet and we wondered whether and how we would get to it. The reality of the moment, indeed of the first two days of our visit, was that we couldn't see apartheid. Very much like home: if you keep to the right neighborhoods, everything around conspires to mask oppression and exploitation. We were wrapped in comfort, actually in unfamiliarly rich comfort punctuated by the black servants seemingly everywhere and sweetened by the rand-dollar ratio that had pegged our excellent dinner at less than $15 for two, including wine.

"So where is it?" I asked Phyllis.

"You mean Africa? I was wondering the same. Where is South Africa?"

"Maybe this is it. Apartheid has been so successful that white Americans, perhaps even white South Africans, feel only its privileges."

"So far it feels no different than being at home."

And we speculated about the ways in which, in our daily lives in Detroit's near-northern suburbs, the racism and poverty that mark American society are equally hidden, as are the ways in which we benefit from them. Perhaps South Africa reflected the same phenomenon, only carried further? Was apartheid as confusing as oppression and exploitation had become back home? The confusion, it turned out, soon dissolved. It was like jet lag, a pattern accompanying us from the United States that faded as our eyes got used to the harsher, clearer light of South Africa.

KwaMashu

A drive to KwaMashu the next day, shepherded by a faculty member of the Social Work department of the University of Natal, punctured the cocoon we had been wrapped in since we entered our South African Airways 747. Even a brief white visitor's tour of this township north of Durban irrevocably makes one conscious that white comfort in the city center is inseparable from black misery beyond the horizon. We knew what to expect from our reading and from American television, yet the reality was still shocking. The desolation stretches on and on and on, and gets worse as the township becomes a shanty town: the two- and four-room houses without inside plumbing, electricity, or telephones; the outside toilets and water taps; dusty dirt roads, barren fields with goats searching for food; few if any public amenities; the tiny handful of cleaning, beverage, and butcher shops; the white-owned shopping center on the outskirts; the unspeakably bare schools running on two shifts with eighty students to a class.

But, as more than one white asked, what makes KwaMashu any different than, say, Saõ Paulo, Brazil? After all, it is no more than a sprawling combination of formal and informal settlements, poor and rudimentary, on the edge of a wealthy city. Does it express any more than the common Third-World pattern of abject poverty alongside, and intimately connected to, extreme wealth? The difference appears when you pass a series of middle-class houses and you are reminded of the almost total absence of amenities that anyone in white Durban, say, might regard as necessary for human life, such as sidewalks or greenery. You realize that this township is a racial city, consciously, deliberately, statutorily planned to be that way. How pitiful these large homes seemed, so much a part of KwaMashu, each one trying as hard as possible to withdraw from it behind high gates and barred windows. Down in the center of KwaMashu a large area was being bulldozed (no doubt at great profit by a white-owned construction firm) to prepare for the implantation of a new middle-class community, a garden suburb within the racial city.

The absence of shops is striking. (I later read that only 30 percent of the shopping of Soweto takes place within the township; 70 percent is done in Johannesburg. On a Saturday, we discovered, one can walk there from the Market to Hillbrow and be virtually the only whites in crowded shopping areas. White Johannesburg, except for shopkeepers, deserts the city, and black Soweto and Alexandra take over.) Its own lack of shops gave KwaMashu a particularly denuded look, a bedroom suburb without a hint of the escape from urban harshness we usually associate with suburbs. This worst-of-both-worlds strangeness suggests the split between the vital areas of black life that go on outside—working, shopping—and are owned by whites, and the far less important (in the eyes of the system) life-activities inside. These activities, such as eating, recreation, sports, child-rearing, education, and health care, are abandoned to blacks without allowing them the resources to carry them out.

One image that stands out is of our guide, assigned by the director of child welfare to show us around the township. This young man, just graduated from the University of Zululand, was gracious and friendly, like all South Africans we met regardless of color or politics. And without artifice. There was in fact nothing significant about our pleasant encounter, except that I was later nagged by the memory of a large hole across the knee of his pants. I felt foolish long afterwards for thinking and wanting to talk about the irrelevant, banal fact that this otherwise neatly dressed young man, wearing a jacket and tie in this first professional job, had a gaping hole at his right knee. Wasn't there something hopelessly first-world about my fixation on proper dress—something chauvinist, even a touch racist? Certainly elsewhere in the Third World, say in Benin or Angola, or even Ecuador or Bangladesh or Burma, poor young civil servants and beginning professionals report to work in clothes that are old, or perhaps used or torn. What of it? Perhaps this cheerful, soft-spoken young man was following the latest style, as one colleague suggested. Or perhaps he had nothing but torn pants to wear to work because of poverty or, as it is now called, underdevelopment?

I rejected seeing his clothing, or the run-down (but immaculate and well-organized) tiny office of his boss, or the desolation of KwaMashu itself, or the poverty of virtually every aspect of black South Africa I encountered, as results of scanty resources or of insufficient development. A tourist can see that South Africa's impoverished townships are planned islands of deprivation within a much larger, well-nourished, well constructed, well-organized, highly productive world. Although blacks make up over 80 percent of the country's population, South Africa has obviously been totally taken over, transformed, shaped, and organized by its white minority. Driving from the University of Natal to Kwa-Mashu takes one past industrial and residential areas, downtown Durban, the high-rise hotels and apartments of Beachfront, and one of the world's busiest harbors. I suspect that one can drive through nearly the entire 500,000 square miles without leaving areas made over by whites in their own image. In this sense there is *no* black South Africa. Even in the homelands one never seems to leave the South Africa that is white-owned and white-developed.

KwaMashu's poverty is emphatically not a result of the persistence of subsistence farming, or village economies, or traditional tribal sectors, but is produced alongside and through a very sophisticated white-owned economy in which each and every South African participates. The township is not a black tribal village (the dominance of Inkatha in KwaMashu notwithstanding) but is rather a *white* imposition on blacks. It is a horrible but thoroughly contemporary part of today's South Africa. That torn pant-leg, assuming it was not a fashion, was mandated not by some rural backwater surviving in the midst of the modern world or by a color-blind dynamic of the marketplace, but by an explicit social decision to house *blacks* in places like this and deny them more than the most meager portion of the wealth produced by a unitary economy.

The deliberate nondesign of the townships reflects a will, a plan, to cripple. Township life, privileged as it is relative to rural black life and "homelands" black life, speaks succinctly about the defiant turn white colonialism took in South Africa forty years ago, its insistence on deliberately and systematically crippling the life of the black majority rather than allowing it to move towards power. At the same moment when all other colonialisms began retreating, the South African one became intensified, creating new townships while destroying places like Cato Manor, District Six, and Sophiatown. In viewing the fruits of this history at Kwa-Mashu and other townships, we learned that their inhabitants are the most fortunate blacks, because they were allowed to remain in these humanly constructed wastelands deprived of amenities, forced to travel endlessly for work, allowed then to work for wages that are a fraction of what whites make. These people are privileged because they live among their families, unlike workers in hostels, and have access to work, unlike many of those further away in the "homelands," where there is little work and even less of anything else. (Fourteen million Africans live in rural areas; the lack of cultivable land forces at least 300,000 wage earners to commute so far that they are away from home at least fifteen hours of every working day.) Also, because it is part of KwaZulu, KwaMashu is "self-governing" and has a certain amount of autonomy compared to the townships of "South Africa."[1] Only a minority of the three or four million Africans who were "relocated"—moved to places like KwaZulu and Bophuthatswana, dumped into the middle of open fields without water, facilities, shelter, or work, and left there to rot and die—are so lucky as to be near work. Hundreds of thousands more live as migrant laborers, passing their lives in hostels far from home and family. And hundreds of thousands more do indeed rot and die.

I will never forget the polyclinic. It is the sole medical facility in this city of 350,000. Open during business hours only, it has ten physicians and nearly two hundred nurses. Another two doctors, and one dentist, practice privately in KwaMashu (the ratio of physicians per thousand is one-fortieth that of the most deprived American state, Mississippi, the ratio of dentists a small fraction of that). After hours, or for a condition determined at the polyclinic to be really serious, patients must find their way down to, and gain admission to, King Edward VIII Hospital, nearly twenty miles south—incredibly overcrowded but the only black public hospital in Durban aside from a new, small one still further south in Inkatha-controlled Umlazi. The scene in the polyclinic was unforgettable because people were waiting everywhere, filling every bench, jammed into every cubic foot of space, waiting patiently, led in singing religious hymns during the lunch hour, waiting all afternoon, perhaps coming back the next day, waiting again.

Here we were again, seemingly back in the middle of the under-developed Third World. In the starkest contrast, in white group areas I kept seeing men and women jogging everywhere. I even jogged myself—up to Cato Manor in Durban, In Mafikeng in Bo-phuthatswana, along the top of an old gold mine in the Witwa-tersrand, along Seapoint in Cape Town. Among whites the most advanced Western health consciousness prevails. I spent a couple of hours talking about cholesterol levels with a disgruntled white Zimbabwean farmer on holiday. What did these people in KwaMashu waiting to see a nurse or to be referred to a doctor think about jogging, or their cholesterol levels? But were these "primitive" people in tribal dress, whose sufferings could be ex-plained by their not yet coming out of backwardness to join the modern world? Children were waiting to die in KwaMashu at that very moment—from childhood diseases related to poor nutrition and lack of sanitary facilities and medical attention. Was this be-cause the foodstuffs and facilities and doctors were lacking in South Africa, or because they were *elsewhere,* by design, by law?[2]

The signs and sounds of KwaMashu, coming on our second full day in South Africa, removed once and for all any possibility that defenders or apartheid might be able to counterpose an "on the other hand" that I would be willing to pay attention to. We could not resist the sense that in this bright morning light we had indeed glimpsed apartheid.

Clarity

Americans who have struggled with their inability to undo their own colonial heritage, of three hundred years of racial oppression, can see that apartheid is an evil beyond equivocation. Because they are racial, apartheid's forms of oppression and exploitation fly in the face of what has become the twentieth-century consensus about the minimal social conditions for human dignity. The United States *and* the Soviet Union both make their claims and criticize the other within a consensus that includes universal citi-zenship in a state functioning for all of its citizens. Only South

Africa, existing as if it were on another planet or in an earlier century, rejects this as a fitting standard. Only in South Africa is the brutalization as widespread, as total, as structural: the vast majority is oppressed politically and exploited ·economically as well as humiliated—by race.

Apologists for the cold war (on either side) paint stark black-and-white pictures of the other side, where grays are required. They give us an evil Soviet Union or an evil America when the realities are far more complex. The unconscious and conscious apologists for power in South Africa function in quite the opposite way: they insist that "the situation is so complicated."

One highlight of my stay in Durban was a flying visit to the Durban commuter train station at rush hour on the heels of a colleague determined to show me how this South Africa was thriving today. In response to my own lecture that day about hope, he wanted to show me that hope was alive and well among South African blacks, that its primary channel was private enterprise, and that government projects, such as improvements in the rail station, were partially responsible. "Here is your hope!" he said grandly, waving his hand lord-like to take in thousands of blacks filing through a vast, congested area. His entire bearing verged on hysteria at every moment. He identified his politics as being pro-government, and regretted that "we" had not cleaned things up in Angola when "we" had the chance a dozen years ago. I suppose his tension came from the fact that he presumed I was anti-government and, worse, was being given a very skewed sense of South Africa by my hosts (who, he proclaimed, would never dare to venture down here in the real world of the Indian Market). In response to any questions about black poverty he complained about American sanctions throwing people out of work, pointed to the mini-van taxis loading up to go back to the townships, and praised their owners' energy in seizing hold of the freedom of enterprise available to them (even though, he lamented, they were bankrupting the bus companies in doing so).

In one of the Indian Market arcades we ducked into a medicinal herb shop. He interrupted the conversation between five Africans by barking out some questions. Everyone looked up, shocked, and slowly took in both of us. Then the shopkeeper, giving him priority, answered. My colleague translated to me from Zulu to English.

"This one is for a headache." He pointed to a short, dark, stubby root.

He swept me out of the shop and we continued, with me rushing to keep up. He stopped others, again lord-like, shouting out questions in Zulu: a black police officer, who suspected my guide of being a plainclothes supervisor; a man carrying a quirt (a cane-length stick) for protection. Each time what fascinated him was the native, the exotic. He delighted in showing me how different from us these people were, and that *he* understood them. Back in the car, he stressed just how different by pointing out how randomly and recklessly blacks crossed the streets, so often causing their own death. "They have no highway sense at all." And then he joked about one such black near his speeding car: "C'mon, hit me. You'll probably bounce back."

His main point, presented at a breathtaking pace and with an unselfconscious colonial bearing, was that here, rare in the Third World, whites had kept things together, and that because of that natives lived with some order and hope in their lives. Compared to the chaos and poverty of Brazil, say, South Africa was a paradise: making enormous strides, providing opportunities, upgrading native life rapidly over the past fifteen years. The whites, it seemed to this man who spread chaos as he moved, had to keep control in order to keep chaos away.

I heard this message at other times, occasionally beginning with a wearing insistence on "just how complicated things are here." The issue wasn't whites and blacks at all, I was frequently told, but the fact that there are so many different black tribes and that they can't get along with each other. South Africa is not dominating its majority, a single black people, but is furthering the development of its many and varied (and indeed mutually hostile) minorities so as to create a genuinely pluralistic society. In mining compounds, for example, blacks from different tribes refuse to live with each other, insisting on socializing only among those of their own tribe. In fact they often fight between themselves. This is why "'one man, one vote' will never work here," and why exotic ways of arranging the franchise and representation are needed to balance the competing claims of the various population groups and keep them away from each other's throats. White minority rule, it turned out, was not a self-interested holding onto power and privilege: it was sheer benevolence, the only way of making this society work.

All the whites I spoke with prided themselves on their own good intentions. Of course, they are right to fear that majority rule may bring disaster. Their way of life may, after all be destroyed: what will happen to their own comfort (so impressive to a middle-class American) if they are forced to pay their servants and workers a living wage? How will they be able to afford architect-designed houses with swimming pools? Can they possibly conceive of submitting politically to people they are accustomed to encounter only as servants and workers?

Their deeply felt arguments on behalf of complexity sometimes threw me momentarily, until I remembered the underlying human, moral, political issue. Then I would reply: "Yes, but morally the situation is quite simple, isn't it?" This was a conversation-stopper. Or I would ask such whites if they didn't feel guilty about how blacks were forced to live. In reply, one man who had earlier in the evening declaimed about black laziness confided to me that every time he heard of a child being killed or saw an old man lying on the street, he would think about his own children and his own parents. It was clear how painted that made him feel. He confessed, with a certain amount of pride, but also in a slightly hushed, illicit tone of someone confessing his secret radicalism, that he had voted Prog.[3] He went on without pausing to speak about the difficulty he would have in pursuing what he, an English-speaking liberal equally repulsed by apartheid and majority rule, evidently saw as the only real solution: emigrating.

One woman, her large diamonds and aristocratic bearing reflecting apparent well-being, echoed a line taken by my guide at the market when I mentioned being appalled by the extremes of wealth and poverty. She replied that conditions in South Africa are no worse than in places like Brazil, and probably better. South Africa, so the argument goes, is a Third-World country, and its inequalities and problems can be explained in terms of "development" and "underdevelopment." Therefore the poverty of KwaMashu or the squatter settlement of Inanda is not a consequence of apartheid, to be tackled best by majority rule (which would in any case destroy the economy), but a world- historical problem no one has yet been able to figure out. Until someone else could manage to figure it out, this woman would continue to enjoy her position at the upper extreme.

I don't know whether such people see anything of black life outside of their employees or servants; but in exploring rural areas, "homelands," and townships, I did not see the "Third World" she spoke of. Whatever may be the case in Brazil, black, tribal Africa, in the *National Geographic* sense of "undeveloped" areas lying outside of the "first-world" economy, is hard to find in South Africa. In this sense, as I said, white South Africa is everywhere.

Bophuthatswana

We journeyed to Bophuthatswana to visit a white couple we had met in London. He was working in teacher-training programs at the university, she in the public schools of Mmbatho. They had moved there to raise their children with blacks and to contribute to black development. Largely apolitical, they hoped to get as far as possible from apartheid without abandoning South Africa. Their house considerably exceeds the already generous standard of the houses of most of our other professional white and Indian South African friends (it is larger, personally designed, and has a swimming pool, its comfort perhaps reflecting the additional pay given to white professionals willing to work in Bop). But unlike every other house we saw it was designed without servant's quarters. Their subdivision is integrated (20 percent black), the only place we saw in South Africa where blacks live legally alongside whites.

After Durban, Bophuthatswana's black "rule" seemed at first to be a relief. Of course, the situation, engineered by the state itself to be confusing, turned out to be crystal clear to almost everyone we talked to. The starkly modern government buildings seemed dumped from out of nowhere onto the dusty fields, giving Mmbatho an eerie, temporary quality. The Israeli-designed sports stadium seemed to belong to another climate, certainly not to the cauldron its windswept plain becomes in the summer. Yet we walked to downtown Mafikeng past streets where the houses of middle-class blacks and whites sat next to each other, saw blacks in positions of authority in the government buildings and shops at the center of town, saw many middle-class blacks clustered together. Was this a hint, however contradictorily, of the human landscape of the future black-ruled South Africa?

Almost no one takes seriously the claims of independence, the priority of tribal identity; everyone mocks the rhetoric of democracy. A black couple we spent time with in Mmbatho was in fact more bitterly opposed than anyone else to President Lucas Mangope, considering him to be a stooge for apartheid, and spoke strongly in favor of total sanctions. After ten years, the original reason why some white idealists originally moved to Bop—to "use apartheid to undermine apartheid"—was now dismissed ruefully. The white South African defense minister and the white head of police public relations, the white former Rhodesian minister of finance, the white South African troops strolling so self-confidently in the middle of Mafikeng, the complete domination by South African corporations—these were some of the easily visible signs of real power.

People spoke of the corruption of Mangope's government and of how he was supported by only a tiny handful. In fact, in a fall 1987 election, the *New Nation* reported that the voter turnout was not 60 percent, not even 6 percent, but .6 percent! In other words, the only voters were government employees and pensioners. Colleagues at the university stressed how repressive the situation was for students and faculty, with the president maintaining iron control and expelling or firing dissidents, with troops occupying the campus. Still, discussing the situation with two white lecturers at the University of Bophuthatswana (Unibo) who took on the air of old Africa hands, we briefly entertained the possibility that the experiment had some substance. We had made our way to the university in a fierce winter dust-storm, and even the faculty offices seemed to be inside a thick red cloud. Cigarette smoke mingled with the dust on a silent Friday afternoon at Unibo as our hosts insisted in apparent good faith that all of the negative signs I reported were inevitable aspects of "Africanization." The huge South African Defense Forces (SADF) men I saw emerge from the gun shop in Mafikeng and drive off in an armored military vehicle called a "Casspir" that morning would have been training Bophuthatswana soldiers. After all, they needed training, didn't they? They had a border to protect, didn't they? It was the most normal thing in the world that such aid should come from South Africa. And so with the whites in high government positions in the black "homelands." Throughout Africa, we were instructed, whites are appointed to key offices *in the interest of black rule,* to avoid factional fights among blacks. As we talked, I felt more and more irresistibly sleepy as the smoke and dust mingled with the sluggish air of these offices and the apparent good faith of these old Africa hands. The truth seemed to have vanished into the dust. Did they really believe what they were saying? These pleasant gentlemen seemed genuinely to enjoy the challenge of teaching their enthusiastic young students—the "blank slates" as they called them—rather than teaching better-equipped white students elsewhere in South Africa for whom the education didn't mean as much (I couldn't help but wonder: Why did they come here? What were their job prospects elsewhere?) And so they would stay here, agreeably, affirming their role in bringing civilization to this backward people.

The problem was that what they said simply didn't fit, any more than the striking government buildings thrown up on vast, empty, windswept fields fit, any more than the stadium designed by Israelis for a Mediterranean climate fit this sunbaked end of the earth. To me that drowsy conversation embodies the political essence of Bop—unreal, even if real people speak the words, even if real people staff it, even if it has real government buildings and real university buildings, even if real blood is being spilled to enforce it.

And yet what of the whites, our friends among them, who are there to get away from apartheid, to live more normally, to do meaningful work among blacks? As in any bizarre situation, beneath Mangope's smiling pictures a few real people are working at raising the skills and the educational level of systematically deprived real people, a few real whites are sending their children to schools next to real blacks, and a handful of real families are growing up on integrated streets. Still, there is the real purpose of Bophuthatswana: to remove South African citizenship, and thus the demand for equality, from three million blacks; to create a pliable tribal leadership totally dependent on white South Africa; to turn the policing of blacks over to other blacks; to further divide and conquer the majority by organizing them according to their tribal identities; to justify South Africa overseas. Within this patently repressive and corrupt political reality it is true that some white and black adults and their children are interacting as other than master and servant. Perhaps, I hoped, out of respect for my friends' work and respect for their sincere desire to live and labor and raise their children alongside blacks, that when the rotten structure inevitably collapses they will then be able to contribute to a nonracial South Africa.

Iscathamiya

I have suggested that South Africa can impose itself with a special simplicity. Seeing invariably involves feeling; the experience that moved me the most took place before our trip to Bophuthatswana and Phyllis's return home. It was one of our few nonpolitical interludes in South Africa, an early Sunday morning when we went off to Glebelands hostel to judge a migrant workers' singing competition (iscathamiya). We were awakened by a colleague's knock at the door of our visitor's flat at the University of Natal before four. We jumped into our clothes and walked down to the little truck driven by the man who organizes the competition. He drove the three of us (my colleague, a scholar of the ANC, stretched out in the tiny enclosed bed for want of sitting space in front) to the Glebelands migrant hostels, south of Durban, on the way explaining carefully how we, the judges, were to operate.

Each group had been practicing since early Saturday night, he said, and when we arrived the formal competition would begin. Tonight was an unusually light night, and we would have to hear only seven groups. They would enter the hall singing a capella and dancing, move towards the stage, and would stop when they arrived at the stage. We were to watch and listen and decide which were the three groups we liked the best. The singers would be dressed "very smart" and each group would be timed to sing for exactly ten minutes once it reached the stage; we could judge them according to how we liked their outfits, their dancing, and their singing—anything we liked, but it was most important that we select three. Yes, I learned, we would be allowed to take photographs and would be allowed to tape the singing. But it was most important that we select the three we liked best.

Whites are asked to be judges (as Indians sometimes are) in order to make absolutely sure of avoiding family ties and thus favoritism. Interestingly enough, it is difficult to find judges, and sometimes the organizer has to go looking and begging at the last moment. Just a few hours earlier we had been to a party with whites and Indians where we discovered that only one other person, the musicologist who had arranged our judging, had been to a competition. If progressive South African whites and Indians had not done it, why were we going? I never for a moment felt any danger, even though earlier in the week the lecturer who took us to KwaMashu had pointedly asked our host there whether we would be safe that day out in the township (we were). I simply supposed that hospitality would make the competition one of the more secure places to be in South Africa. The more pressing question had to do with what it would feel like to be whites sitting in judgment on black singers in South Africa. I thought with discomfort of the whites who had driven up to Harlem in the 1920s for a taste of the exotic, but I knew that I would love the music, and, as our host explained how we were to function, I realized that the whole experience would be sufficiently formalized to protect the sensitivities of all concerned. We later learned, in fact, that we had made a hit because we were so serious, taping with our cassette recorder and shooting with our camera.

Entering Glebelands, I was struck by the gate that guarded the entry; although no one was now on duty, I suppose any "unrest" would immediately produce guards to oversee who came in and went out. This is repeated at smaller townships: a single, controlled entry point that everyone has to pass through (in townships the police headquarters may sit behind bunkers and barbed wire alongside the entry point). Everywhere in South Africa are such reminders that the state is at war with the bulk of its population. Obviously some of the security precaution is clear self-protection, such as the bunkers surrounding police stations, or bunkers and barbed-wire fortifications around oil refineries and storage depots. Some of the precautions, however, seem political and psychological, designed primarily to foster militant fear in the white population towards the threat of black liberation—such as the routine body searches at enclosed shipping-center entrances and the large posters graphically picturing the weapons of ANC terror.

The second striking image of Glebelands at four o'clock in the morning is the hostels themselves, which our host assured us were "very good." Compared with what I saw later they were indeed very good, but viewed from the outside these long red brick buildings, jammed with migrant workers living away from their families, two or four to a room with toilet and cooking facilities down the hall, eleven months a year, seemed rather bleak.

The recreation hall, a former church, lay up a hill past the hostels and beyond a couple of shops, one of which was owned by our host. He parked and led us into the hall, directly to a table set off from the small audience and placed at the front of the room facing the stage. We were offered refreshments but declined, and began to set up our recorder, note pads, and camera. We were a bit uncomfortable, but we were above all curious and excited about being there.

After a short time the first group came out, and was marvelous. They wore matching brown suits with string ties, which made a stunning contrast with their leader's grays. Perhaps it was simply the thrill of our being there and of hearing them first, but we were enormously moved by everything they did: the interaction between group and leader, the singers' steps, their rhythms, the rich, varied, somewhat heavy and slow-paced medley. It turned out that almost every group moved beautifully, was dressed smartly, sang with great discipline and polish, and was thoroughly enjoyable. The music was unfamiliar, but the tonalities and the chant-and-response pattern were generally not. I must confess that we had biases. We were less impressed (or were even annoyed) by deliberately American stylings or direct appeals to the judges (some groups moved directly toward us, sought out eye contact, and deliberately courted us), and tended to favor sounds that seemed to our untutored ears to be more artistic and authentically African.

As the competition continued we compared notes, informally ranking the groups in relation to each other. Even so, it was disconcerting that we kept finding ourselves favoring the group that had just performed over all the previous ones. Was it the performance or the singing we liked best? Or the dress or the music itself? As I now listen to the tape of these aspirants to be the next Ladysmith Black Mambazo, I hear why it was so difficult: certainly five of the seven groups were good enough to be ranked first.

When the last group finished, the organizer drew the curtains and placed a blackboard on a stand in the center of the stage. The words "First," "Second," and "Third" had been painted in white directly on the board, and I was given chalk to write the numbers of the groups once we had decided. We deliberated for a while and, surprisingly, took a relatively short time deciding to rank the first, fourth, and seventh groups as the top three. (The organizer later told us that the fourth and seventh groups win frequently, but that the first group had never before won.) I went up and wrote their numbers on our board and, after I had sat down, the organizer opened the curtain with a bit of fanfare and announced the winners, to general applause. Then what was apparently a spontaneous celebration broke out, with members of the winning group and the third group gathering on the stage to dance and sing, along with their girlfriends. We were thanked by the organizer and he led us out to the daylight and his little truck.

The comforting distance imposed by the judges' table dissolved somewhat as we walked out. Just before we got in the truck, a woman standing with several others came up to me and said, in broken English: "Baas, please, baas, please. I need work. Five rand a day, two rand a day. Please." We tried to explain to her that we were not South Africans, but were visiting from Detroit, where they made cars, in the United States. Eventually, I think, she understood. As we drove off we turned to her and her companions, and exchanged waves.

Pain

In playing the tape, today, months later, I feel once again the emotion that percolated just beneath the surface while we listened to the competition in Glebelands, the emotion that finally clarified South Africa to me. It is an emotion whose intensity had been keeping me in the fog since returning—I seemed unable either to leave it behind or to recover it in this American setting. Purely and simply I felt pain, pain for those migrant laborers lodged there, by apartheid, in those red brick blocks of rooms. I felt pain, and feel it today, for all of the victims of apartheid I met—those in hiding, those whose family members have been killed, those who have been detained, those who claim things are better than ever and don't want to rock today's boat, those who live and work in the townships, those who must control their rage at white arrogance, those who go door to door to beg for work or a few rand to feed their children, those who (like the man who fetches mail for the department I was lecturing in) have corrupted themselves and others by exploiting white guilt and regularly "borrowing" money from employers, those who keep getting moved around by the state, even those who stole my jacket from a lecture podium at the university while I was talking to students. I feel pain for those "Asians" who continue to be humiliated by being second-class citizens, as well as for those whites who courageously act against apartheid and become swept up in all the tensions of their apostasy but who also remain oppressed by their own sense of guilt.

This pain hit *as pain* at Glebelands and not in conversation or at KwaMashu. It has been slowly, silently growing, and probably was sharpest at Glebelands because there we didn't have to defend against it. Music does that. What we noticed first about the singers was their smart outfits, no doubt saved up for over weeks, bought with money withdrawn from other survival needs, perhaps from sums sent back to families in the "homelands." And then we were struck by the beauty of their singing—the talent and skill and discipline and energy of these people who have been forced to live as less than people. Here, probably without saying so, perhaps even out of escapist and apolitical fantasies of stardom, they were triumphing over the system's definition of them and creating their own self-definition, giving to us who were so privileged to hear them the beauty and hope they had been shaping for months, even years. These battered and humiliated boys and men, crammed into these brick boxes, sang above all of their grief—of being away from home, of missing their loved ones. They did it so beautifully and captivatingly that for the space of time they danced down the aisle and the ten minutes, precisely, each group moved across the stage they seemed to shed the victim state and escape apartheid. And because of the beauty and hope of their music, we allowed ourselves to feel purely, plainly, and clearly our own accumulated pain at the victimization from which this beauty grew.

Intermingled with the music's hope and joy we were probably feeling our feeling, not theirs, our reaction to apartheid, not theirs. I am not sure how far we actually experienced them, the Jabula Home Defenders and the six other groups; perhaps all that happened was that their singing permitted us to release to consciousness what we had been feeling, and suppressing all along, about South Africa. Wasn't it this sense, that apartheid is a burning issue, and is making specific people suffer brutally so that other specific people can continue to live well at their expense, that drove everyone we spent time with to continually talk about the situation? I suspect that even an Afrikaner I argued with on the flight from Cape Town to Johannesburg, who begin by saying "they're inferior," was aware of the suffering apartheid causes its victims. I think South Africa is living a collective pain, made an issue by the movement for majority rule, and that it was perceiving this that made my encounter with apartheid so powerful. This anguish binds together all those who oppose the system and suffer from it, and strangely enough it sometimes binds together people on opposite sides, even including the Afrikaner racist who reluctantly admitted how hurtful the state is.

And so, unwilling and unable to cushion it with ambiguity, I came to experience South Africa through a single set of lenses: white oppression of blacks. Was I avoiding the full complexity of South African reality? Of course. Did I oversimplify it? Of course. But I think one has to find one's way to perceiving the stark oppressions of apartheid—and the attendant simplifications are a fitting first response.

I was able to perceive and feel this clearly not only because I was a visitor but, equally, in spite of all ambiguities, because things are clear. I was privileged to be able to experience the urgency that initially accompanies such awareness, and to be able to throw myself into the situation and engage myself with every breath and bone in my body. Paradoxically, because of the fullness of this involvement, I felt a rare intensity during my stay in South Africa. Its source was the distressing simplicity I have been describing. I experienced apartheid through imperatives that are at once moral and political: that blacks must rule, will rule. That they are right. It is simple, and hastening their day is a clear, pure, compelling duty.

Part Two

Intervening

3

Responsibility and Complicity

A white American professor, especially one carried along by all the pressures of an academic visit to South Africa, tends to move around among whites. From the beginning this made me uneasy, and I had to make a sustained effort to meet and interact with blacks. But it also meant that I "naturally" spent much of my time among members of the minority whose privileges apartheid was designed to protect. Yet I saw only a corner of that world, largely English-speaking liberal and radical academics and other professionals. Some of them are among those who oppose apartheid, "but—."

In the process of arguing against their passivity before what we always agreed was a horrible evil, I heard and tried to rebut many of the excuses used to justify inaction against undemocratic, unequal, and exploitative societies everywhere. How is it possible, I asked someone occasionally, to acknowledge the evil of a situation, benefit from it, and not feel driven to act against it? Were they the "good Germans"?

Parallels with Nazi Germany are irresistible anytime South Africa is mentioned. This is partially because describing it provokes the need to think and speak hyperbolically. The most inhumane society of the first half of the twentieth century is invoked to describe the most inhumane one of the second half. Since Nazi Germany springs to mind as having committed the worst crimes imaginable against humanity, critics of South Africa easily fall into such comparisons. Moreover, more than one scholar has noted real parallels between the two societies (see chapter 5), making such links all but irresistible.

But, after all, the differences are decisive. The Nazis hated and destroyed the Jews; they entertained visions of world conquest and a thousand-year Reich. Moreover, they were a vast majority. White South Africa regards itself as besieged and engaged in a primarily defensive battle, against people it claims not to hate and in fact depends on economically. Genocide is the furthest thing from its mind. While the Nazis' "Final Solution" seems to have no basis in what we usually think of as self-interest, apartheid is flagrantly a system of privilege and of labor control. Much of white South Africa seems to have benefited materially from the transformation of black South Africa into one vast work camp.

Nevertheless, the parallel persists. Both social realities exude evil; in the most simple sense, of being organized so as to systematically attack the human essence as such. In the one case killing factories were set up to destroy a people; in the other, there is a system of social engineering in which one people denies another some of the most basic attributes of what it means to be a human being today. Both societies are universally condemned as violating even the minimal human standards of their critics in other oppressive societies. At the same time, one was, and the other is, an established constitutional society: anti-human policies were, and are, carried out in the name of the majority of citizens, and with their obvious acquiescence and even support.

Talking with white South Africans made it clear that they had thought about, and agonized over, this fact. I dealt with it twice in lectures, once to staff and students in the department of German at the University of Natal, the other time to a class in political ethics at the University of Cape Town. By and large I was speaking to "good South Africans" who oppose apartheid, "but—" and my goal was to argue that *they* are responsible for the situation they detest. As a Holocaust scholar and a student of Sartre, I developed most of the following argument in those lectures, and then afterwards filled in my references as well as some of the blank spaces. The main points are not original but, above all, it is a response to South Africa developed on the spot, trying to provoke people to think about their own role.

To Those Who Oppose Apartheid, "But—"

Irresistible questions call out to a philosopher of the Holocaust visiting South Africa today: Who is responsible for this social system? How can we assess responsibility for such evils?

My reflections begin with another question: Who is responsible for the extermination of millions of Jews and others at places such as Auschwitz and Treblinka? This is a major question in its own right, as well as for the light it can throw on how to deal with this most urgent of centuries. Do the institutions and instruments of the modern world function increasingly, as some claim, to hide individuals from responsibility for their own acts?[1] Does individual responsibility dissolve more and more into relationships of obedience to higher authority?[2] How far can we extend the accusation of complicity with actions taken by a tiny handful? Was the Holocaust only the beginning of a series of more and more streamlined horrors divorced from their agents, leading us to social systems like apartheid on the one hand or a truly *final* solution to the *human* problem on the other?

When we try to understand why apartheid continues, we confront a modern social system that has been relegating tens of thousands of children to die of starvation each year—in one of the world's rich countries. For years the South African state has remained in power in the name of a little over half the country's white population and in the face of worldwide condemnation. Can thinking about responsibility for the one horror, the Holocaust, give us insight into who is responsible for, and how to stop, the other, apartheid?

It is odd to still be assessing responsibility for the Holocaust forty years afterward. After all, it has become the most infamous of historical events, mountains of documentation and writing about it have accumulated, and it is kept prominently before the public consciousness. Still, great confusion exists in the public mind, even now, about what responsibility for it means and exactly who was responsible.[3] And this confusion clouds our understanding of South Africa.

According to the charter of the International Military Tribunal at Nuremburg, "Leaders, organizers, instigators and accomplices participating in the formulation or execution of a common plan or conspiracy to commit [crimes against peace, war crimes, or crimes against humanity] are responsible for all acts performed by any persons in execution of such plan."[4] As regards the Nazi extermination program, a handful of people seem to have made the policy and drawn up the plans to implement it. Their responsibility was relatively easy to decide. Tens of thousands carried it out but only obeyed orders: are they responsible? The SS guards brought to trial since, such as Ivan "the Terrible" Demjanjuk, are usually only those thought "guilty" of extreme brutality. The overwhelming majority of the tens of thousands rest peacefully today, fearing neither apprehension nor judgment.

Beyond them, hundreds of thousands more were indispensable parts of the machinery making the exterminations possible, but most of them never touched a living, or even a dead, victim. Some handled the victims' eyeglasses or assayed their gold rings and teeth; some inventoried their property or carefully recorded their names and numbers. They would deny responsibility even more vehemently than those who have been brought to trial. Are they responsible? The problem is not only that virtually everyone involved has denied responsibility. Beyond the very careful and intelligent courtroom discussions of the actual degree of culpability of the major actors and the cruellest guards[5]—a tiny circle of actors—the world has felt no need to clarify just what it means to have been responsible for the Holocaust. Clearly, the overwhelming majority of the guards and of the bureaucrats will live out their lives unnoticed, implying that, beyond the key Nazis and the sadistic guards, no one else deserves to be brought to trial.

Perhaps we can be helped by the "muddled" thinking of those who refused to buy Volkswagens. There are probably still a few Jews today who will not buy German cars; the phenomenon was widespread in the 1950s and 1960s. Were all Germans responsible in fact? Or is this an imprecise, overgeneralized "lesson of the Holocaust," understandable as the instinctive reaction of the first generation, but fortunately now mostly forgotten by their children?

I would argue the contrary, that the blanket rejection of things German, like today's blanket boycotting of things (and people) South African, contains two thoughts which demand our attention. First, the Holocaust was the policy of the legitimate government of Germany, was carried out through the use of all the resources of Germany and in the name of German society. We are warranted in holding Germany responsible for it even today, to the extent to which the Federal Republic of Germany is a successor regime one of whose goals has been to ensure the easiest possible transition from the Nazi period, retaining in positions of political, economic, and social power the very people and institutions who kept the Nazi government functioning and refusing to come to terms with its past.

But should we spread this to all levels? All officials? All agencies and corporations? A second useful thought contained in the blanket condemnation of Germany is that hundreds of thousands, even millions of "good Germans" made the Holocaust possible. They are part of the web of institutional functioning, ideological support, and political complicity without which Jews, and others, would never have been slaughtered. And linked with that web, and permitting its function, was the rest of German society, all those who, in Karl Jaspers' words, "went right on with their activities, undisturbed in their social life and amusements, as if nothing had happened."[6] Coming to terms with this vast web remains the unfinished business of the postwar era. Muddled as it may have been, the thinking that seemed so principled yet idiosyncratic in rejecting German cars challenged the forgetfulness of the first generation. And it suggests that another vast web of complicity today supports apartheid.

We know, in some way demanding clarification, that the web of responsibility for the Holocaust extends beyond those few who have been brought to trial—but just how far? Jaspers, for example, insists that "each one of us is guilty insofar as he remained inactive."[7] What does it mean to be responsible? It is worth noting that, while briefly exploring this theme in the *Nichomachean Ethics,* Aristotle does not concern himself with our modern question, suggested by Jaspers, of who is responsible for the actions of a state. Although he discusses what it means to hold an individual responsible for his or her own acts (for example, was the action voluntary or done under constraint?)[8] Aristotle seems light-years from our characteristic concerns: What is the responsibility of an individual acting, with others, for his or her nation-state? What is an individual's responsibility for actions directly produced elsewhere in a complex division of labor in which he or she participates? The point is that these are peculiarly modern questions. They historically presuppose not only the emergence of the individual as ethical subject—largely the creation of Judaism and Christianity—but also the modern nation-state and its conception of citizenship as a relationship between that ethical subject and the larger community.

It is in today's world that responsibility becomes an issue. It does so in two peculiarly modern ways: when ethical subjects deny their responsibility for evil acts that they have clearly committed, ascribing them to the nation-state structures that commanded them; and when individuals who themselves do not act directly are accused of supporting and making possible the evil acts of other individuals. In the first case, the individual denies ethical responsibility for an act he or she actually performed, dissociating him- or herself from the consequences of his or her own act by claiming that he or she was not acting as ethical subject but obeying a command or carrying out a role imposed by the state. And the second case involves holding the individual responsible for an act he or she did *not* commit—because in aiding and abetting it, he or she in fact made it possible.

"I was only obeying orders"—this is the claim giving rise to the first question. Jean-Paul Sartre has sketched a sweeping, nonetheless effective, reply: by deciding to obey them, I have made the orders, and all acts springing from them, my own. An early statement, in *The Emotions,* characterizes the unchanging core of Sartre's thought: "For human reality, to exist is always to assume its being; that is, to be responsible for it instead of receiving it from outside like a stone."[9] I am "condemned to be wholly responsible for myself."[10] The extermination-camp guard is in effect told that he or she always retains ethical subjectivity, and is always free to evaluate whether orders are right or wrong, legal or illegal.

By now Sartre's argument on this first point has largely won out. In the wake of the Holocaust, this issue has been resolved. Since 1945 humanity collectively seems to have amplified the meaning of citizenship by deciding that every individual has the responsibility to subject every state's every order to the scrutiny of conscience. States will want to deny this, and to punish individuals who insist on disobeying. But from governments to the military to political activists to philosophers a kind of international consensus has grown up—extending to the American war in Vietnam, for example, and the Israeli invasion of Lebanon, as well as the Israeli suppression of the Palestinian Intifada in the West Bank and Gaza—arguing that it is correct, and necessary, for individual conscience to evaluate orders ethically before carrying them out. For our purpose this means a growing sense that the individual citizen is responsible for every act he or she carries out. Thus the Vietnam War saw anti-conscription campaigns in the United States; the invasion of Lebanon and continuing occupation of the West Bank and Gaza have seen movements refusing specific forms of military service in Israel; and the state of emergency, continued occupation of Namibia, and intervention in Angola provoked the End Conscription Campaign in South Africa. Sartre's central claim has triumphed: soldiers, and everyone else, cannot pretend that any of our own acts, whoever may command them, can be divorced from our own will and subjectivity.[11]

The second issue remains less clear, however. "I was only a clerk." Or: "I did not know it was happening." Or: "I disapproved but was powerless to stop it." In these cases we are dealing with people accused of complicity. As Richard Wasserstrom points out, the charter of the Nuremburg tribunal casts

a very wide and fine net of responsibility. Given, for example our assumption that [in Vietnam] the United States is involved in the commission of crimes against peace, war crimes, and crimes against humanity, all members of the armed forces as well as countless civilians appear to come within these principles of responsibility. And the principles of the responsibility of coconspirators and the criminality of group membership appear to extend the range still further.[12]

On the one hand, this would suggest that even induction into the American military in Vietnam was to be rejected on the grounds of "vicarious liability" for a "conspiracy to commit the crimes against peace, war crimes, and crimes against humanity" committed there by the United States. On the other, as Wasserstrom notes, "There was simply no thought, in the minds of the draftsmen, when they used admittedly sweeping terms, that ordinary conscripts into the German Army would be held liable for accepting induction." Nor, later, in the minds of the judges. Ordinary soldiers were "never prosecuted or blamed simply for having served in the army."[13]

Why not? we may ask. It seems as if the sweeping principles of responsibility and complicity—the "wide and fine net"—were meant morally, and perhaps rhetorically, but not politically or legally. I would suggest that the contradiction between principle and practice does not mean that the Nuremburg tribunal was being hypocritical. Rather, it was being realistic. It would have been inconceivable to try to prosecute all of those who were sincerely thought to be complicit in Nazi crimes. It would have raised questions well beyond the prevailing legal notions of criminal responsibility and guilt. The kind of vital moral-political questions asked by many young Americans, Israelis, and South Africans in the years since—for example about a conscript's responsibility as a member of a larger, evil system—were simply not the kinds of questions we would expect a postwar victors' court to be asking.

If the rhetoric and practice of the Nuremburg tribunal on the question of the ordinary soldier's or the ordinary citizen's responsibility are thus confusing, perhaps the sweeping claims of Jean-Paul Sartre will guide us in clearing up this confusion.[14] Of course, Sartre's incautious rhetoric will put off many people. His essay on anti-Semitism, almost exactly contemporaneous (1944) with the Nuremburg War Crimes Tribunal, sounds like the underlying rationale for not buying German cars: "In this situation there is not one of us who is not totally guilty and even criminal; the Jewish blood that the Nazis shed falls on all our heads."[15] But more is involved here than Sartre's characteristic verbal extravagance, whose goal is to provoke guilt and then action. Thomas Flynn points out that this essay probes "the social climate, the entire value system which is oppressive of Jews" (55). As Flynn says, Sartre "is implying that in an anti-Semitic society each of us is responsible for anti-Semitism to the extent that we permit or even support those bases and structures which make possible the choice of anti-Semitism" (57).

But how are we responsible for the evil done by others? Sartre does not answer the question in this essay, but he pursues it over the next thirty years in plays, in essays on French history and, significantly for the parallel with South Africa, colonialism and neocolonialism, as well as in his biography of Gustave Flaubert. As we have just seen, he begins with claims that are so total that many critics have regarded them as meaningless—if we are all responsible for everything, it has often been said, then we are equally responsible for nothing. He then stresses, as in the case of French colonialism in Algeria, and specifically in the case of French soldiers using torture during the Algerian War, that not only the settlers but all French citizens are directly responsible.

By plunging us into a despicable undertaking, [our political leaders] have invested us from without with a *social culpability*. But we vote; we have cast ballots and in a way we can retract them; a drop in public opinion can bring ministers down. We must be personally a party to the crimes which are committed in our name, since it is in our power to stop them. This guilt which has remained inert and foreign in us must be assumed on our part—we must degrade ourselves so as to be able to bear it.[16]

Colonialism, Sartre stresses during the Algerian War, is a system. Not only is every settler implicated in that system and responsible for its evils, but so is every citizen of the metropole. After all, "the pioneers belonged to you; you sent them overseas, and it was you they enriched."[17] His claim casts the widest possible net even as it becomes more precise: "All of us without exception have profited by colonial exploitation."[18] As Sartre later points out, it will not do to plead that this happened before we were born: the current generation shapes itself through the structures bequeathed it. It must combat the evil of this inherited colonialism or it accepts it as its own.

"But I did not know it was happening." During the Algerian War Sartre wholly rejected this as the same kind of bad faith used by the Germans in 1945 to evade their collective responsibility (the kind dismissed by Karl Jaspers).

At that time it was not proper for the German population to pretend to have been ignorant of the camps. "Come now," we used to say, "they know everything!" And we were right, they did know everything; and it's only today that we can understand it, for we too know everything. Most had never seen Dachau or Buchenwald, but they knew people who knew others who had perceived the barbed wire or consulted confidential memos in ministries. They thought as do we that the information wasn't sure; they kept quiet; they distrusted each other.[19]

Of course not everybody knew exactly what was happening. Later Sartre will stress that complicity need not involve knowing every detail or indeed even specifically knowing about massacres themselves. To be responsible for the massacres of French workers in 1848 it was enough to share the class-identity and class-project (we may add today race-identity or national-identity) of those who ordered and carried them out. Thus one might have shared Nazi anti-Semitism, given it personal support by repeating anti-Jewish lies or jokes, or even simply tolerated it. Or less: one might have simply identified with the Nazi party and its project. Such a person may not have approved or even known about the murders at Auschwitz, but (to directly apply Sartre's analysis of the French bourgeoisie in 1848): "*He carried them out.*"[20] He did not carry matters to their logical, brutal conclusion; it was enough to have shared the premises and goals of those who did, to identify with and support them.

The remainder of Sartre's analysis of serial responsibility in 1848 fits Nazism exactly and may be directly applied, with the change of a single word. The typical Nazi supporter, we might say, did not go to Auschwitz,

but this omission was accidental (a matter of distance, difficulties of communication, personal reasons); but he was there as Other; here, he was afraid; *there,* in the person of some other, he was proud in his [Nazi][21] courage. This identity in alterity ... nevertheless continues through events of which he is still unaware: tomorrow he will learn that he has killed a man. (*Critique,* I, 761; Flynn, 160)

He is responsible even if his action is passive and serial—perhaps involving no more than paying taxes, serving elsewhere in the Army, belonging to the party or even having voted for it; or perhaps simply cheering Germany on in the war and contributing his sons to it; or perhaps simply accepting passively an atmosphere of anti-Semitism, violence, and Führer-worship.

And so, given the appropriate modifications, with South Africa. Certainly Sartre's approach remains sweeping and lacks precision. It can hardly be true that "if you're not victims when the government which you voted for, when the army in which your younger brothers are serving without hesitation or remorse, have undertaken race murder, you are without a doubt executioners" (Preface to Frantz Fanon, 25; Flynn, 64). Granted you are complicit, and may later be judged guilty, but to what degree? Sartre is not interested in answering this, and so, while moving towards a systemic analysis of complicity (for example, laying stress on the crimes of French imperialism and capitalism), he has little eye for laying bare the simple, material, everyday links between the "good Frenchmen" and the brutalities committed by their state.

As we do this, we must be careful to situate Sartre's analysis, and our own efforts, in history. With all due respect to Sartre, a citizen's responsibility is not an ontological fact, but a social and historical one. Human beings as such are not always and everywhere equally responsible for acts carried out by their rulers, whether or not in their name. In talking about Aristotle, I said that such responsibility belongs above all to the ethical subject who is the full citizen of the modern nation-state. Definitively torn from localism or regionalism by the modern nation-state, our modern citizen/ethical subject, already the product of a complex historical process, was then thrown into world history. Although the process has taken place unevenly, we have all come to live economically, ecologically, politically, and militarily in one interdependent world. We are all aware, for example, of Americans' or South Africans' real links with places like the Soviet Union or Britain or Japan. Alongside these relationships of interdependence sits another: we live as citizens of nation-states that are modern mass societies, demanding our allegiance and specific forms of more or less active support. The political process has been taking place more unevenly than the development of our economic interdependence; South African blacks, for example, are scarcely responsible for the actions "their" state takes towards them. And we must speak of degrees even among those with full citizenship rights: an American or a white South African has greater effective political rights, and thus greater responsibility for his or her government, than does a Soviet citizen. Moreover, virtually all contemporary governments claim to act in the name of their citizens. The citizenry's actual degree of responsibility for their government's acts may vary from regime to regime—only participatory democracy in a classless society would involve full responsibility. Nevertheless, it is important to note that while Sartre himself usually had in mind Western parliamentary democracies, his most horrible example of individual guilt was Frantz von Gerlach, torturer, citizen of Nazi Germany. Responsibility is thus not limited to those with the right to vote in a parliamentary democracy.

In thinking of responsibility for the Holocaust or apartheid, and in what ways, we must combine Sartre's insistence on responsibility—which he usually describes in absolute terms—with a sense of degrees and of concrete ways of being responsible. We can conceptualize this by thinking in terms of a *spiral*. The spiral of responsibility moves outward: from those who conceived and ordered the Final Solution, to those who acted on their behalf and planned and directed its every detail, to those who directly laid hold of Jews, shipped them to places like Auschwitz, and once they were there, directed and ordered them into the gas chambers. The spiral then includes hundreds of thousands of others who supported their actions by acting elsewhere in the division of labor, at hundreds of points in the machinery of state, those who belonged to the Nazi party and so gave its projects political force, those outside the party who voted the Nazis into power, those who opposed them but passively acquiesced in their being voted into power, and finally those outside of Germany who did nothing to stop the nightmare.

As we have already seen, there is little controversy today about the inner circle of perpetrators. Or about the next turn of the spiral, consisting of hundreds of key people who actually ran the machinery of destruction (in a list containing the names of a "few," Raul Hilberg lists about three hundred high officials and indicates their fate).[22] Or the next turn, which contains the tens of thousands of Waffen-SS concentration-camp guards (Hilberg estimates them at fifty thousand [576–78]) who physically staffed the machinery, as well as the perhaps ten thousand administrators.[23] All of these people acted as vital components of the machinery of destruction. Above all, they *were* the machinery of the Final Solution, each one occupying a necessary post in the division of labor which alone made possible the extermination of European Jewry.

At the center of this spiral is Hitler himself, master of Germany, originator of the Final Solution, the man who gave the order. But those who actually carried out the Final Solution were deeply committed Nazis. Even if they claimed to act out of obedience, they accepted Hitler's authority, they accepted the unreason entailed in such a choice, and they accepted as well the movement's specifically violent, revanchist, anti-Semitic, racist, antidemocratic politics. The step of obeying Hitler cannot be separated from the substance of that obedience, the man's spell over them from their acceptance of the intentions implicit in that spell.

But how deeply does the spiral extend into Germany, how far beyond those who directly bloodied their hands? The next turn includes hundreds of thousands: not only the soldiers and SS troops who rounded up Jews and shipped them to the killing centers, but also those who expropriated their property, the clerks who catalogued it, the construction workers and railroad crews, the police, physical, and administrative apparatus outside of the camps that made possible the grisly work going on inside.

Beyond these people are all those who put the Nazis in a position to carry out the Final Solution or contributed to the climate in which it became thinkable. For example, the next turn includes hundreds of thousands who, in the years before the war, carried out the multitude of tasks which led up to the Final solution—from those who broke Jewish store windows and boycotted Jewish businesses to those who staffed the administration that removed their citizenship. After the war many of them argued that the anti-Semitism of the 1920s and 1930s was one thing and extermination quite another, that they supported the first without having any inkling it would lead to the second. At the next turn are the members of the Nazi party who may not have participated actively in its anti-Semitic acts, but who joined and supported the party—for other reasons, perhaps, later claiming to have ignored its anti-Semitism. Next are all the rest of the fifteen million Germans who, not Nazis, voted for the party in the July 1932 election. And the additional four million who voted for it in 1933.

On the next turn are all those "good Germans" who, while disliking the Nazis and sensing the evil and madness of Hitler and his movement, failed to mobilize themselves to block the Nazis' rise to power. Once Hitler was in power they may have continued to oppose silently, but they paid their taxes and gave themselves and their sons to the war effort. About them, Sartre is right: those who are responsible include all those who did not fight the regime, or shield Jews, or go into exile and fight Nazism from there. We now know today that the spiral does not end here. It continues beyond Germany, to those Allied leaders, and their administrators and political supporters, some of them Jewish, who knew about the extermination camps but failed to order or push for their destruction. They did not cause the Holocaust, and perhaps were not what we could usually regard as complicit in it; but they did not take action to stop it.

"What else could they have done?" This question may be asked on behalf of Jewish leaders in the United States who sensed no alternatives to going along with the national consensus about winning the war as rapidly as possible; it may equally be asked about the guards who, under military orders, participated in shipping Jews to the camps. "I did not know what was happening in places like Auschwitz." This may be argued on behalf of all of those who, in Germany itself (the extermination camps were in the East) had the vaguest sense that something terrible was happening, but knew not what. "I supported Hitler, but not extermination." This would be the statement of many who voted Nazi but rejected the consequences of Nazi rule. "That was the Nazi policy. I was just an ordinary citizen, not a Nazi." This would be the claim of the passive, apolitical "good" German.

The idea of a spiral of responsibility answers these objections by stressing that, while it took millions to create and accept the conditions that led to the Holocaust, each of those responsible contributed in a specific and definite way, and is responsible in a specific and definite way. All of those who accepted it and allowed it to happen are responsible for it, and all of those who carried it out are responsible for it, and all of those who ordered it and planned it are responsible for it—but in different ways, and to different degrees. Broadly speaking, we may think of four large categories of responsible persons: those who command and act; those who carry it out; those who are actively complicit (in several ways and degrees); those who are passively complicit (again in several ways and degrees). A complex division of labor itself creates these degrees of responsibility.

Sartre is wrong: the "good" German is not *as responsible* as Heinrich Himmler. The one passively went along, kept his or her ears closed,[24] grumbled silently against the Nazis; the other actually directed the apparatus. Certainly any effort to assess responsibility gains by seeking to clarify how and in what way people are responsible, but does it not lose by weakening some people's sense of responsibility? I suspect that Sartre understood that any efforts at precision might alleviate the discomfort he sought to provoke, and so he instead argued more sweepingly, for virtually no distinction between accomplice and torturer. Thus his inflammatory language: "without exception"; "totally guilty and even criminal"; "on all our hands"; "know everything without a doubt"; "executioners."

The fact is, however, that no matter how far we look, we never see more than a few key actors carrying out the Final Solution. Most of the fifty million Germans remain accomplices to varying degrees. But to call people accomplices does not necessarily mean letting them off the hook. In fact this exonerates no one; rather, it tells us a great deal about how the modern nation-state operates. Once the Nazis controlled its machinery, they required only a relative handful of obedient servants to operate it. Once political hegemony is won, only a few are needed to carry out genocide. And Hitler's main victory, unfolding over the ten years before January 1933, was to win power. This required the active or passive consent of millions, indeed, tens of millions—the strength of some, the weakness of others. Each of the supporters may have done very little, or even nothing. But each did precisely what was required of him or her.

In this sense, even when partial, responsibility is absolute. The average "good" German was certainly no more responsible for the Holocaust than the average "good" American for the near-destruction of Vietnam. But no less. In the complex modern state, catastrophe can only become policy if each of us does our precise part—as workers, as party members, as citizens, as bureaucrats. Indeed, the policy-makers count on it. Where people refuse to do their part, as did tens of thousands of Danes when orders came to ship away the Danish Jewish community, the destructive machinery grinds to a halt. Danes withdrew their tacit approval, their passive compliance, and assumed fully their responsibility for Danish Jewry—and saved them.

Even when partial, responsibility is absolute. How does this reflection on Nazi Germany apply to the vastly different situation in South Africa today? Shifting from the past to the present exposes a confusion we have operated with until now, one between responsibility and guilt, and perhaps another within responsibility itself. On the one hand I have been seeking merely to examine one situation and determine how it took place—to describe the specific roles played by all those who may be regarded as active or passive participants. This effort to assign responsibility is a matter of description. But it implies a second operation: the ascription of moral responsibility. The Nuremburg tribunal, after all, was concerned with guilt. At issue was knowing whom to punish, and how severely. More recent discussions of "German responsibility" are intended, if not to punish, then to lay the moral stigma for the Holocaust at the door of all those who were to blame and, at the very least, to provoke serious reflection among and about them.

But this cannot be the purpose of our discussing responsibility for apartheid today, especially when the ANC is so generously reaching out to the ruling minority. Its goal is to build bridges towards the dominant whites, to lay the basis for future reconciliation—not to assign guilt. As Herbert Fingarette points out, a concern for guilt focuses on the past. "Guilt is retrospective, but responsibility is prospective." The act of determining guilt concerns itself with something that is over and cannot be changed. Sartre's extreme language, I have suggested, is not intended to provoke guilt about the past but rather action in the present. And that is the concern of this discussion. As Fingarette puts it, "Responsibility is based on a willingness to face the world as it is *now* and to proceed to do what we can to make it the world as we would like it to be. To accept responsibility is to be responsible for what shall be done." [25] This leads us from the past, the Holocaust, to the present and future—today's struggle to end apartheid. The point is to describe responsibility within a very specific framework, of asking what shall be done by those who share in the evil.

Whether we are speaking in moral terms or in political terms, the question is, insofar as the system oppresses specific human beings, who is responsible? The many-layered spiral of cooperation of the modern South African state moves outward from those at home who perform and command to those, even overseas, who profit or acquiesce or even turn away. Let us look only at those who mean well, English-speaking whites and Americans.

One feature of my every conversation with English-speaking South Africans has been their denouncing of apartheid. A second has been their blaming it on Afrikaners. Some of the reasons emerge in discussion: group areas, population registration, and other features of apartheid are policies of a state dominated by the Nationalist party; apartheid was implemented by this Afrikaner party after it rose to power in 1948; the Nationalists not only gained control over the legislative and executive branches of the government but also populated virtually the entire bureaucracy with Afrikaners and even created a vast Afrikaner-run network of public and semi-public businesses. Today, so the argument goes, it is the Afrikaner who maintains apartheid. The English-speakers who oppose it are a minority among the whites. "What else can we do?"

This stress on Afrikaner responsibility is a bit distortive. As National Union of Mineworkers leader, Cyril Ramaphosa, has pointed out, if we may distinguish between an Afrikaner political ruling class and an English-speaking economic ruling class, most of the features of what became apartheid were introduced under the British *well before* the Nationalists took over political power. British mining capital benefited greatly from the extreme low wages paid to blacks and the system of labor control. As recently as 1979, G. W. H. Relly, the chairman of Anglo-American Corporation, declared that, in gold mining, "Migrant labor is here to stay . . . and should be accepted as a permanent feature of our economic and social order." [26]

Certainly, as Merle Lipton has convincingly shown, since 1948 the large corporations have opposed key features of apartheid—the pass laws and other forms of labor controls, the heavily interventionist state, the various ways of subsidizing white labor—as being destabilizing, in violation of human rights, and destructive of their own self-interest. And equally certainly, they have tried, with the means at their disposal, to modify state policy on these issues. But within limits: the Afrikaner newspaper *Die Burger* once poked fun at the English who "joined the Progressives, voted for the UP [United party], and thanked God for the Nationalists." Today, a good half of them vote for the Nationalists. In other words, in the present as well as the past, the limits of English liberalism have always been framed by a deep interest in political stability and defense against the "security threat." Even if, as Lipton describes it, a kind of surly "minimum consent" rather than wholehearted white unity "prevailed within the oligarchy," [27] this common "minimum" commitment was, and is, to white economic and political power. Thus the English have remained, and continue to remain, ambivalent and contradictory on the ultimate issue, full political rights for blacks.

The fact is, however, that those who today inherit and profit from an economic and social system, and who operate decisive aspects of it, are responsible for it—even if they oppose parts of it, pressure a state they dislike for limited changes (while continuing to accept the state's determination to hold power), and finance changes designed to undermine it "eventually." Hundreds of thousands of white South Africans vote for anti-apartheid parties, hate the system, yet live exceedingly well because of it and above all *do* nothing else against it. Their electoral opposition to apartheid is itself equivocal to the extent that the parties they vote for have not yet called for majority rule in a unitary South Africa.

Sartre, and our sense of the modern state, can guide us to describe these whites: their government allows them to grumble, to perform charitable and educational acts, and to vote against apartheid. And it tolerates, and from time to time even yields to, their pressures to change certain aspects of the system. Like any modern state, it insists only that, in their central political relationship to it, they not actively oppose it in ways it has defined as being beyond the pale, that they pay their taxes and collaborate in its structures and actions. Rather than "collaborate," why not say "acquiesce," as Lipton does in describing so well the difficulties faced by the English opponents of apartheid?[28] Why suggest an active rather than a passive complicity? Because the stronger term suggests the fact that they are privileged by the system—economically, socially, and politically—and that they still accept, and operate according to, its fundamental premises. They benefit from the system and remain a loyal part of it. And the system is built on the subjugation of blacks.

Sartre's sweeping absolutism is illuminating: everyone born into it, living within it, benefiting from it, is responsible for it. Meaning not that they should be consumed with guilt about it, but rather that they should ask themselves how to fully assume their responsibility for it. Only those acting against it, rather than remaining loyal to it, have faced their responsibility and transformed the complicity into opposition. They act to create a *different* future, on their own behalf and on behalf of those oppressed by the system.

This ascription of responsibility may extend across the Atlantic, but does it reach beyond the American government offices and corporate boardrooms? Certainly we Americans are not *as* responsible; a sense of degree is needed. And our direct benefit may be minuscule in the larger scheme of American corporate profits which, as we know, are shrinking even further where South Africa is concerned. But look at our concrete links: we Americans elect a government whose political support, many analysts think, has become absolutely essential to the survival of the Nationalist government. Current irritations and tensions aside, in the long run South Africa's constitutional arrangement would not survive the kind of pressure the American government is quite willing to place on, say, Angola, or Nicaragua. Grudgingly against apartheid, the American government remains no less of an ally of the South African state than ambivalent English-speaking capital has been a partner of the Afrikaners in the South African oligarchy. In giving decisive

support to the South African state, in taking its leaders as colleagues, however errant, rather than as enemies, the American
government acts in the name of the American people, and with the
passive support of that people. Like it or not, we Americans are
part of today's spiral of responsibility for apartheid. The links are
there, whether we choose to see them or not.

This does not by itself impose any particular political course,
either vigorous corporate intervention to develop black skills and
authority, partial or total disinvestment and/or sanctions, or even
military aid to Umkonto we Sizwe.[29] It is worth insisting, however,
that the political analyses seeking to decide this question must distinguish the various participants' manifest intent, as shown in the
totality of their actions and these actions' effect, from the stated
intent. In other words, if we avoid being swept away by their
words, what is the *net* effect of their involvement?

Answering this question inevitably involves connecting it to the
actual political forces in motion; improving black education by
bringing blacks into a few elite integrated private schools is a worthy goal, for example, but should its supporters remain passive
while black opposition is hunted down and detained?[30] Can they
withhold support for the specific organizations in which the opposition is organized and still consider themselves opposed to
apartheid? Helping black students prepare for their "matric" (university entrance) exams or upgrading the skills of domestic servants is a good thing to do. But should those who sponsor such
programs consider that they have thereby effectively opposed
apartheid and fly in the face of the demands of the major black
opposition organizations, by lobbying mightily to make sure foreign arms keep flowing to the state? The tone of Sartre's irritating
absolutism can remind us: the point is not to support both sides,
as do American corporations which donate both to Democrats
and Republicans or South African corporations which support the
state *and* oppose apartheid,[31] but to decide which side one is on,
and to act consistently with this decision.

These particular complexities, and evasions, were scarcely possible during the Holocaust. In the totalitarian, genocidal landscape
of Nazi Europe, *any* action an individual took is today respected
and even honored: hiding Jews, slowing down the machinery of
destruction, actively opposing Hitler politically, joining the partisans. Today's "yes, but—" would have been impossible in 1943.

Thus does history itself define moral alternatives and their meaning. Nevertheless, it would be wrong to conclude by conceding that "the situation is so complicated" in South Africa today, as do so many who follow "yes, but—" with these words when they speak about ending apartheid. It may be possible to argue about different paths to it, but ultimately all questions in South Africa flow from, and can be distilled back into, a single issue, the question of power. Who will rule South Africa? In the future, people will be assigned their final places on the apartheid spiral of responsibility according to whether their actions today hastened or retarded the shift to majority rule.

4

Hope and Action

Although cautioned to "stay out of politics," I was invited to South Africa specifically in order to give the Richard Turner Memorial Lecture. Turner was born in Cape Town in 1941. After attending the University of Cape Town and taking an honors degree in philosophy in 1964, he enrolled at the Sorbonne, where, under the guidance of Jean Wahl, he took his doctorate. His dissertation studied political implications of the philosophy of Jean-Paul Sartre. Returning to South Africa to teach in 1966, Turner found a permanent position in 1970 at the University of Natal, where he was known as a provocative and popular teacher and a fierce opponent of apartheid. First married while still a student, he was divorced in 1970 and, in contravention of the Mixed Marriages Act, married a "colored" woman the same year. He was actively involved in political work, which included developing a close relationship with Steve Biko, organizing a program of research on conditions in factories, and establishing a journal of labor affairs. Under the terms of a 1973 banning order he was prevented from leaving Durban, from attending gatherings, from entering factories, union halls, or the university, and from publishing. Over the next five years the University of Natal continued paying his salary, and he engaged in a reappraisal of several major philosophers from a point of view seeking to integrate the insights of Sartre and Marx. In January 1978, two months before his banning order was to expire, he was assassinated by an unknown gunman. To honor the memory of Richard Turner, the University of Natal established a memorial lecture in 1986.

After my first few days in South Africa, I became aware of the need to talk to those who were following in Turner's footsteps. I wanted to honor the memory of someone whose writing had illuminated South Africa for me, and whose spirit, life, and work had left an unforgettable impact on many people I met. I had also come to sense the exhaustion and resignation of many of those I had become closest to. Not that they had lost hope. Indeed, witnessing their persistence in the face of overwhelming power is one of the most heartening experiences I have ever had. But in the current climate of repression they persist often routinely, by shutting out their expectations, because they feel they must: equally refusing to give up, on the one hand, or, on the other, to take heart from anything they have already accomplished or their connection with the rest of the world. Many of them, in other words, keep on plugging, intentionally adrift somewhere between hope and despair, obstinacy and exhaustion, feeling and numbness—not at all in the spirit of Rick Turner. My lecture sought to do what many of them have decided is impossible—to ground hope, to formulate a way of keeping it alive and present. As with the previous lecture, I here clarify and develop my argument.

To Those Who Struggle against Apartheid

In reading Richard Turner's *The Eye of the Needle* I discovered him to be a comrade as well as a colleague. It is a wonderful book, simultaneously moral, theoretical, committed, clear, alive. Tony Morphet, in his moving introduction to its second edition, claims that *The Eye of the Needle* is not Turner at his best. Perhaps so. I can only wonder about how good his best must have been. *The Eye of the Needle* is as useful today as when it was first published, displaying a genuine unity of value, theory, and practice in its reflection on the situation in South Africa. I have also come to know Rick through many South Africans who were deeply affected by him. Ironically, perhaps the greatest tribute came from the then minister of law and order, who (with typical racism mixed with fear and anger) called Richard Turner "the most dangerous man in South Africa." Richard Turner thought, he acted; he led, inspired, challenged and shamed others into thinking and acting.

Rick Turner was unusual, of course, in that he was white. That the liberation movement has seen many black martyrs—from week to week and day to day it sees many more—is no surprise. A people fighting for its own liberation expects to be set upon by identifiable agents of the state, by commando forces outside the country, and even by unknown vigilantes. But it is less common that those raised to a life of privilege are willing to give up their privileges in order to spend their lives struggling on behalf of the aspirations of the majority. I take Rick Turner both as the specific individual who goaded and inspired many of you and as symbolic of all the many, black and white, who have lost their lives in the struggle for a free South Africa.

A situation in which those struggling for majority rule are detained and banned, are beaten and murdered, is truly one in which we must ask ourselves about hope. Is there reason to hope today? Such questions begin with our continuing sense of loss for Rick, even after ten years, and our daily and continuing sense of loss for the other victims of South Africa's death squads—people destroyed for their commitment to the most basic human values. The assassin's bullets that cut Rick down in front of his daughters show how fragile hope, and the people who dare to live and act by it, can be.

At the end of my first public lecture in South Africa I deferred answering my opening question about whether there is reason to hope today. I wanted to show just how difficult it is to keep up hope, in South Africa or anywhere else, and tried to do so by dwelling on the extraordinary irrationality which has more and more come to be considered as normal in the twentieth century. I asked whether the situation in South Africa, today, indeed, since the Nationalists began implementing apartheid, has gone far beyond what we might consider to be rational—if oppressive—self-interest. "Are they too crazy to cut a deal?" was the final, unanswered question. That is, are the powers that be too irrational to face reality, to see the handwriting on the wall, and to calculate how to preserve as much as they can? If so, catastrophe impends.

Which is, of course, one reason why hope is in question in South Africa today. It is in question everywhere. Alongside the many catastrophes of the century, catastrophes we have still not fully absorbed, further catastrophes lie in wait. And not because movements or politicians are simply mistaken, or ignorant, or defending untenable privileges. Or caught up in what Barbara Tuchman described as "folly." It even seems to be an objective trend. Disaster beckons more and more, as political and social groups choose the irrational, the impossible, consciously and deliberately flying in the face of reality. The South African state president boasted recently that he had only used one-tenth of the power available to him to crush unrest. Presumably, he still has nine-tenths of it at his disposal, loaded, lubricated, waiting to be fired!

Although my generation was brought up believing in human prog-ress, in the slow victory of Enlightenment principles, in an irresist-ible movement towards equality and democracy, we have learned that such sinister boasts as that of the president are not rhetorical. It will be a disaster for South Africa and the world if all of this power is used. But it may well be. Viewed against the century's background of disaster, such determination gives us profound rea-son to lose hope.

If hope is in crisis today, one response must be to study objective political and social tendencies, in South Africa and elsewhere, to see, concretely, what basis they give us for hope. But because it is so deeply and systematically besieged, the subjective human trait, hope, itself demands clarification. That is my purpose here. Hope demands interrogation into its nature and structures and condi-tions, a philosophical reflection.

What is it, hope? What is its place in the human world? How is it sustained? I am talking about the structures of a general subjec-tive attitude, one that can become a concept and then a way of life and even a philosophy of history. Such a broad starting-point is necessary because we begin with equally broad questions. Is hope to be understood individually and/or collectively? Is it tied to our own activity, or is it a passive expectation? Twin children of the Enlightenment, Marxism and bourgeois thought solved these problems by building hope into their evolving conceptions of how the course of history itself was unfolding. There was no need for a separate reflection on such "subjective" attitudes as hope be-cause one could *smell* the smoke of Manchester or *see* the march of science, or *witness* the building of class-consciousness. Today, on the contrary, a century and a half of history's unfolding after the codifications of Karl Marx and Auguste Comte, we must dis-entangle hope, like so much else, from a catastrophic century and a menacing present, in order to ask what it is and whether and how it may be sustained.

The Nature of Hope

First of all, what is hope?

There are many possible hopes, probably an infinity of them. They include specifically individual and everyday ones, such as my hoping that it won't rain, that I'll get all of my work done, that I'll make ends meet this month. There are also specifically political ones. For example, if *Time* wonders, "Are there signs of hope in South Africa?"[1] they have some very particular hopes in mind. Will there be a softening of, and then an end to, white domination—without social transformations that would endanger the climate for American investment or remove South Africa from the American ideological camp? Can South Africa fulfill its role within the American world order? Will there be an end to disruptive conflict?

This is not the hope I'm talking about, the hope worth asking about philosophically. It is, rather, inherently limited, partial, and narrow, springing from a highly specific project. *Time,* of course, will try to convince all of humanity to accept its specific hope, acting as if it were the self-evident human hope. One goal of all ideology is to persuade as many as possible into taking a specific, narrow hope for universal human hope. The editors of *Time* know: to be worth talking about, hope is for human beings *as such*. To ask, "Is there reason to hope today?" poses a general question directed at a universal audience. The question wonders out loud about our collective lot. It asks about universal values.

What do we hope for then, really? What do we hope for as *we?* First, to avoid the worst. Nuclear war threatens all of us. South Africa is faced with prolonged and deepening agony. We hope to avoid these. And then, inevitably, we hope for more: the peaceable kingdom, a condition of well-being and harmony. *Harmony* suggests social peace based on mutual respect. In the historical world of the late twentieth century, this means ending the most oppressive forms of domination. The United Nations Universal Declaration of Human Rights captures this by demanding dignity for *everyone* in the most concrete of ways, allowing for meeting basic aspirations of each. Perhaps this can only be done, we might add, in a situation which refuses to privilege the aspirations of any.

This last, sweeping qualification may give pause, because it so runs against the grain of what currently passes for political thought in the West. Let me be clear: I am not at the moment talking economics, whether capitalist or socialist, but hope. But I am talking against the ideological fantasies concocted by those who desire to continue privilege and domination while avoiding their intrinsic, inevitable conflicts. Let me continue to be sweeping: hope prefigures an egalitarian world, even, I would suggest, a democratic and socialist world. This is because to hope, I would argue, at its fullest and deepest, involves coupling individual with collective well-being, and forecasts empowering those who have been powerless and ending a history in which the poverty and impotence of many has been a condition for the well-being and power of a few.

But what about purely individual hopes? Certainly, we must distinguish between individual hopes and universal hope. But as Ernest Bloch describes in *The Principle of Hope,* most of the deepest, most meaningful personal hopes are about, or at the least are profoundly conditioned by, the individual's relationship to the world. It is a foolish or a blind hope that denies one's intimate interdependence with the rest of the world. Moreover, to hope for oneself alone while the world is going to ruin or, indeed, to hope without regard for others, is, I would suggest, secretly to despair. We are, after all, situated in the late twentieth century. Today, strictly individual hope, whether in South Africa or the United States, is to eat, drink, and be merry if you can, haunted by a profound sense of impending doom. It is blindness rather than hope, a desperate wager that no one actually notices your private celebration. This is why Bloch suggests that individual hope, at its deepest and most authentic, sets its sights on universal well-being. Conversely, the general hope entails the individual one as well. We ask not only, Will the world improve? but along with it, Will my life finally get better? Will my children's lives? As Bloch makes abundantly clear, hope is above all collective, but in inseparable connection with individual hope.

Certainly the dominant thinking today in the West runs against this claim. It may grudgingly concede that we all live in a global village, but it insists that the only possibility of meeting the aspirations of each is to allow free rein to a few—allegedly to "generate" the social wealth that will not only reward them but "trickle down" to everyone else. On the contrary, the logic I am asserting, and suggesting is a deeper logic, runs counter to "free-enterprise" hope. I am arguing that individualist ideology is an attack on hope. "Free" enterprise pretends to speak of "the" individual but beneath its rhetoric has in mind a *few* (and indeed, a specific few) individuals. Its social system works, as its victims know, to generate the well-being of a few at the expense of those upon whom this well-being rests but who do not really benefit from it. Benevolent as they can be made to sound, privilege and domination, set free, really want themselves, not general well-being. And they never seek to undo themselves. For all their old-fashioned simplicity, even Reagans and Thatchers cannot abolish sunrise and such simple truths. On the contrary, hope, if it is *our* hope, collective human hope, requires a different vision, one seriously concerned with universal well-being. Because universal well-being implies equality, this kind of hope, as Bloch knew, envisions a new society.

Reaching *harmony* implies achieving a peaceable kingdom, one which does not have to defend domination and scarcity, one which is not consumed with rebuilding after the apocalypse. But hope further means arriving at this general well-being without the kind of catastrophic destruction that would make its goals unachievable. It means avoiding mortgaging the new society far into the future, as Vietnam remains mortgaged, and will remain mortgaged, by the destruction exacted by forty years of French and then American resistance to national liberation.

Hope and Progress

In the larger historical picture, hope has emerged as tied to the idea of progress. In questioning the viability of progress in 1966, Theodor Adorno still had not given up the aspiration "that things will finally get better, that one day human beings will be allowed to breathe easily." [2] If, as Bloch suggests, human beings cannot live without hoping, until the modern world this hope often found collective expression and refuge in religion, "the heart of a heartless world" as Marx said. Approximately two hundred years before Adorno, beginning with the French *philosophe* Turgot, hope was first secularized. Although this young abbé initially set his thought within the requisite theological framework, the father of the Enlightenment concept of progress effectively removed hope from the realm of religion. Turgot claimed that life was getting better, here on this earth and because of human efforts. He stressed the cumulative character of human knowledge, and the inevitable improvements it would usher in. Just as God and other-worldly hope were being shown the door, the West ushered in a secularized, social, political, material hope: the belief in progress.

According to what was to become the dominant bourgeois conception developed two generations later, that of Auguste Comte, an individual had to do nothing but allow the world to get better by itself, virtually on its own, inevitably. Once bourgeois society was freed from artificial restraints imposed first by feudalism and then democracy, science and technique would increase mastery over nature and augment productivity. One had only to submit, to join his or her life with the larger historical process. According to the Marxist conception, on the contrary, progress was taking place dialectically, in struggle, involving political and social as well as technical and economic transformation. Still, Marx sometimes echoed Comte's mood of inevitability. The individual was expected to join and contribute to the larger movement of social transformation leading to a classless society. The Marxist conception, without mentioning progress—probably dismissed as a bourgeois idea—was in fact the zenith of progress. Coupling social progress with plenty, it was the highest of hopes yet elaborated, forecasting the beginning of history, when humans would finally control their world.

The experience of the twentieth century, however, has dimmed these specific hopes, and above all has dashed the sense that large historical forces are making human life better and carrying us along with them. For example, look at how contradictory progress has been, and how much it menaces us. Compared with Turgot's period, life today may be better for some and in some ways, but it is also worse in other decisive ways and for many. Is the lot of black South Africans better or worse today than before the encounter with Europe? If the question is answered on the plane of lived daily life and not future hopes, every gain can be countered by a loss, until the list of the losses continues well after those who would speak of gains fall silent. For example, as Immanuel Wallerstein argues, modern capitalism developed racism as an "oppressive humiliation which had never previously existed."[3] Most of its benefits to the Third World are, alas, still only "potential" ones.

In the twentieth century we have been forced to learn a rather unsettling truth. There is no automatic process of human advancement spiraling upward, whether operating dialectically or not. Catastrophe is all around us. How then, can we have hope? In South Africa and the United States today, the answer is the same no matter how different the situations are. Hope does not come from waiting for the machinery of history to move forward. Indeed, the only machinery that seems to move on its own—but does not, really—is that furnished by science and technology, by the state, capital, and the party bureaucracies. The career of such machinery gives us no reason to rest assured. Today, Comte's approach—to free, and then wait on, inevitable forces—courts disaster. As anyone in Africa should know, progress at best was always ambivalent, as destructive of the many as empowering of the few. It was inseparable from the project of Western domination of the non-European world. To preserve hope today, everywhere in the world but especially in Africa, does not mean waiting for forces like progress to make life better. If it has any meaning today, hope means something drastically different than it did to Turgot or Comte, or to Marx in his mood of inevitability.

Hope and Action

Today, here and everywhere, keeping hope can only mean acting. To hope means to *create* the possibility of a better future in the face of stalemate or even impending disaster: intervening directly, politically, to try to make a future that is better than the present and its dismal trends. There is truly no hope without action.

And it means action of a specific kind, action towards universal well-being that becomes concerted, conscious, and collective. The larger world, and most of its specific societies, is not moving towards ameliorating the struggle for survival. Considering its managers, and the way they have engineered its machinery, it will not. Those who wish it to, can preserve hope only if they assert that wish as a political project. In a century of accomplished and impending disaster, to keep hope alive can only be done through active intervention in the name of "making things finally get better."

Today, just as hope is individual *and* social, so does it forbid us waiting on events. But isn't this qualification fatal? Marxism, for example, makes little sense without at least speaking of larger social tendencies towards revolutionary transformations, towards liberation. Today, thrown back on the rudimentary principle of action in the face of menacing, destructive trends, we must ask: Are things tending to get better? Do we have concrete reasons to believe that our action will succeed?

The point of stressing action is to force us to recast these questions. To put it most starkly, in its two-hundred year career, secular hope has been based on the assurance that positive trends were unfolding objectively all around us. To insist on action as the first principle of hope is to concede that this is no longer true, to live without such prior assurance, to agree that today action must produce its own justifications. Because history has turned out so badly, I would suggest, in the United States as well as in South Africa, we should all try to see ourselves as potential Rick Turners, or, more to the point, as among the thousands of black and white martyrs of the struggle for majority rule. I would suggest that we should try to see ourselves as the Jews of the Warsaw ghetto: watching as our kinsmen are shipped away, waiting to see who will be next, wondering when our turn will come, some of us even feeling the inevitability of disaster. To understand hope today, I am suggesting, we must reject all triumphalism. We must begin not by thinking about progress or positive trends or tendencies, not by assuming successful outcomes, not by assuming history is moving as we would like it to. Instead, let us look at the action of those trapped in extreme, even impossible situations, for example, the action of those who become combatants.

Action and Human Values

In the spring of 1943 in the Warsaw ghetto, action against the Germans was obviously not undertaken to achieve victory. It was done to assert humanity and dignity in the face of conditions that all but destroyed the meaning of being human. It was done to reject passivity and submission, to deny the Germans an easy victory. And as an act of solidarity with all those fighting against the Germans. An underground leaflet proclaimed months before the uprising: "Remember that also you—the civilian Jewish population—are at the front in the fight for freedom and humanity."[4]

When I say that, today, this kind of action is at the origin of hope, I am not speaking about just any action, or action for action's sake. Nor the action that anticipates victory. Rather, it is moral-political action that asserts vital human principles about the way things ought to be, for example, by overturning relationships of oppression and domination. Ought: such action reminds us of the great ideas and values, the great ethical and religious traditions. To take only the example of Rabbi Hillel, who lived during the time of Jesus, responding to a challenge to reduce the whole of Jewish teachings to what could be said while standing on one leg: "Do not unto your neighbor what you would not have him do unto you; this is the whole Law; the rest is commentary." Philosophically speaking, how do we justify this idea? Is a universally valid morality embodied in the great traditions? And if so, how do we extract it from situation-bound or invalid themes? I would suggest that answering such questions is the province of the history of ideas—tracing the evolution of culture-specific ideas into more and more universal ones, and following the slow development, in social and political struggle, of an effective human social morality that more and more reflects these ideas. Ideas of how things "ought to be" have slowly evolved in various writers and traditions. Such theories have developed and broadened and deepened, and collective human action has tended to make them clearer, more insistent, more definite and universal. Our notions of human dignity today are fuller and more articulated than the earliest ones, with which they remain continuous. The historical process itself has redefined and refined the meaning of being human, all the while expanding it, and has created the material and political conditions for actualizing this in human social relations.

Accordingly, to hope today is to act on behalf of the human best. And this can be, has been, articulated. If it begins with good versus evil, light over darkness, right over wrong, in time it has become further specified as cooperation over aggression, universal rights over particular privilege, solidarity over self-aggrandizement, a higher social morality over individual self-seeking and aggression, democratic rule and majority rule over minority domination. This list becomes more historically specific because we human beings have, over time, specified human social morality and human dignity ever more concretely, developing and placing on the agenda such ideas as concrete demands of specific people in specific societies. The Freedom Charter summed them up for South Africa in 1955. Today, indeed, some insist that it needs further specifying. In South Africa or anywhere, then, hope has the concrete meaning of acting on behalf of the highest, most humane, most evolved values and practices of our civilization, sighting the fullest vision of human development over its lowest, crudest, most primitive practices and principles.

But even if I am suggesting that there has been definite progress in articulating and achieving more humane social relations, this is not due to the historical process moving by itself. It is only and everywhere the result of specific human activities, above all, of social struggles. Movements seeking greater human dignity have sometimes been victorious, but they have sometimes been defeated. Today many of them remain stalemated: the liberation struggle in South Africa; the struggles of blacks and women in the United States; the struggle for democracy in Poland. And if we contemplate the Warsaw ghetto uprising or the life and death of Rick Turner, we stare at a defeat and destruction so shattering as to cancel all triumphalism.

Still, defeat at a given point and time is not decisive. Today, the combatants of the Warsaw ghetto are seen by all humanity as having been right, their victimizers as having been wrong. In an odd but profound sense, the Ghetto fighters have won. Their victimizers have been defeated. Yes, of course, both fighters and victimizers were destroyed, but world morality today says that *they*, the combatants, were right. The Nazis killed almost all of European Jewry but they failed, utterly and totally, to redefine them as evil or subhuman. In the wake of disaster, this is an unexpected, but no less a positive, lesson of history.

Political repression can victimize tens of thousands. The total detention figure in South Africa since 1984 is at least thirty thousand people. The human cost has been enormous, but these people's assertion of a higher vision of humanity cannot be detained permanently. They can be smashed, be set to fighting among themselves, be discouraged. But like Rick Turner even in death, the vision stands there waiting for new exponents who will give it its day. It moves among us, always voiced by someone, now no more than a gadfly, now an irresistible movement.

Consequences of Action: Breaking Complicity

Hope: we break with the passivity that demoralizes; we connect our individual aspirations with collective aspirations; we act on behalf of the highest morality. Some of us survive massive defeat and discouragement and wait to renew the struggle on more propitious terrain. And, sometimes unexpectedly, changes follow. I quote Isaac Deutscher, quoting Lenin, quoting Napoleon: First,

we must decide to act and then we *see*. Once we engage ourselves
the fact of acting itself illuminates the situation, changes it, and
changes ourselves. For example, action changes the situation's appearance of inevitability. Any specific evil appears inevitable and
overwhelming when we are discouraged by it, or if we regard it
passively, as separate from ourselves, on its own. It appears as
simply there, an independent force. But once we are engaged, or
become re-engaged, *against* it, this evil becomes redefined as something to be combatted, the enemy. We see it in relation to ourselves
and our actions. We see ourselves affecting it, it responding to us.
We contest it, looking for its vulnerabilities, acting against them.
Just as the evil changes in the process, so do we too change, now
empowered by the struggle.

Active in struggle, we are changed by becoming moral agents.
In overcoming the demoralizing and corrupting split between belief and action, in deciding that we can abide the situation no
longer, in throwing off our discouragement and passivity, in refusing to be overwhelmed, we break our complicity with the oppressive system. In all of these senses we destroy the modern state's
peculiar hold over us. In the South African context, I especially
have in mind the complicity of anti-apartheid whites who do nothing against apartheid but grumble. We may recall that the Nazi
death machinery operated by requiring only a few to carry out its
commands. The rest, "good Germans" perhaps, may well have
hated the Nazis, they may have grumbled, but they did what was
required of them: nothing. In the United States the Reagan nuclear
escalation flew in the face of opposition by 60 percent of those
surveyed, as the more recent American effort to destroy Nicaragua
has flown in the face of opposition by over 50 percent of those
surveyed. But these passive majorities fail to translate themselves
into active majorities, or even significant active minorities, who
might stand in the way of carrying out policies they dislike. Instead they become complicit by giving the state, passively, in precisely the way required, all the support it needs to carry out the
vicious policies of a minority.

In South Africa today such complicity yields undeniable privileges to its white beneficiaries. But passivity towards apartheid is
worse than a Faustian bargain. It means accepting evil policies
done in one's own name. Unless one challenges one's own privilege—not by giving away one's possessions but by opposing the

system itself that sustains privilege—one bears that corroding responsibility for its evils. Breaking with it, to put it most simply, is to do the right thing. Becoming morally active is one of the greatest liberating experiences. No matter how many times we come up against this argument and try to get around it, there is really no way of escaping the American New Left's most provocative statement of the 1960s: You're either part of the solution or you're part of the problem.

Consequences of Action: Joining a World-Historical Movement

As I have suggested, moving toward action also enables us to see the situation in a new way. By engaging ourselves, we redefine the situation itself. I have spoken about the impulse to action, the determination that creates hope, as resembling the acts of a Rick Turner, or of the combatants of the Warsaw Ghetto. We act because we must, to assert our humanity, to do what is right, without any guarantee of success. Such action has a further consequence: acting on behalf of social justice joins us with a world-historical movement.

In South Africa today, however, many people speak of majority rule as "inevitable." Is this a sign of confidence in how it will turn out? Actually, I would suggest that this statement is an appeal *against* a present that seems to utterly deny it. But what kind of argument does it make? On the surface a demographic sort of political argument (How can the vast majority be kept without political rights?), it is really an appeal to a vast world-historical process. The "inevitabilities" are that colonialism and racism *must* end, that majority rule *must* triumph. But why is this inevitable? Obviously, if it is, this is only because over time, specific human beings themselves have abolished first one then another specific form of domination and oppression. Indeed, the history of humanity, so often seen as a story of increasing alienation and powerlessness, seen today as an anti-progress, can also be written from the point of view of the gradual rise of human dignity and the gradual softening and abolition of various forms of oppression. It can be written from the point of view of a movement that reaches back to before Spartacus and the Roman slave revolts and forward to the local campaigns against removals in South Africa today, to mass movements in Warsaw and San Salvador.

Before we get carried away by triumphalist rhetoric, it is important to ask: Can we speak of "a movement" for a process so complex and many-sided, whose components are unrelated and even contradictory? Yes, because even if we would speak of specific movements, isolated geographically and separated in time, some striking facts impose themselves on us. We see their results accumulate in each separate society, becoming new bases upon which future movements construct new demands. Once successful, the struggle over slavery in the United States never has to be repeated; nor will the struggle for black political and legal equality; nor will the struggle for women's rights. No, blacks and women have, not yet achieved equality, and the resistance to de facto equality takes subtler, more sophisticated forms as the de jure inequality erodes. But even as we bewail how far ahead stretches the road still to be traveled, we must not forget to glance back and see just how much has been won. Often the very complaints themselves signify positions won, voices trained, constituencies listening—achievements that have emerged only as hard-won fruits of struggle. Furthermore, each society and each struggle is increasingly less separate from others. Movements and their victories inspire each other, one success (for example, the American Revolution against British rule) encourages both the demands and the expectation it can be repeated elsewhere (the French Revolution a few years later).

Perhaps it is straining to speak of a single worldwide movement (although in 1968, such a "movement" certainly existed); what we see in this global village is rather a complex many-sided movement-in-the-making with victories, great monuments, with traditions, with heroes, and with martyrs like Rick Turner. And of course, with defeats. Its various strands tend increasingly to make similar kinds of demands, and to build on the accumulated victories achieved elsewhere and in the past. And above all, these victories, over thousands of years, have led to distinct and measurable advances in human social morality.

One such advance is that virtually the entire world has abandoned, has had to abandon, the belief in hierarchy based on race. This has happened in the context of a still larger struggle against some of the privileges based on birth, a struggle on behalf of certain universal human rights. "Some," "certain"—the fact that so much injustice remains, is not even considered injustice, does not make the worldwide condemnation of South Africa into an aberration. It is not cynical, and it is not hypocritical. In the United States and Great Britain, South Africa is seen as an anomaly because, with all due reservations, a higher level of social morality has slowly, painfully been achieved in these societies. Everyone born in these countries is regarded as a citizen, regardless of race; every citizen is statutorily guaranteed full political, civil, and human rights. Universal citizenship, with whatever its limitations, is the norm virtually everywhere in the world, and a society refusing to grant this in the late twentieth century is regarded as a moral and political monstrosity.

How have such results been achieved? Certainly they have not been due to the solicitude of the privileged. Rather, they were produced in the same world-historical movement that is demanding change in South Africa today. Everywhere they were granted only after prolonged and costly struggles. Even in South Africa, the past fifteen years have seen significant if not yet decisive changes. Why? Because of the relentless struggles of millions of people. And these have not been isolated from other struggles, elsewhere in the world.

In deciding to act, in South Africa or anywhere else, it is important to see, feel, and experience solidarity with the world-historical movement-in-the-making which, over thousands of years of history, has not only destroyed the fact and even the possibility of slavery but has begun to destroy other practices of social inequality, has extended education to hundreds of millions of people, has achieved formal democracy and civil rights nearly universally. Even in South Africa, one of the apparent exceptions to the rule, the pressure from other societies, their victories and the norms that have resulted, act on us all, inspire us, and will continue to do so.

The individual commitment I spoke of earlier, that existential moral commitment, thus joins a world-historical movement reaching back thousands of years and increasingly to every corner of the world. The ethical plane of my argument joins the philosophy of history as I speak of this large, cumulative process as being an effort, increasingly a single effort, to make these many struggles into one struggle. For in the process we more and more insist that movement-in-the-making will not remain as just another trend of history, as it is currently, but will rather become *the* meaning of life and the meaning of history.

The meaning of history? If the movements continue, and coalesce into a movement, it may yet become apparent: the long, slow, painful process of creating the possibility for dignified human life, for personal, political, and social power, for everyone. This, I would suggest, is the ultimate goal of hope.

Consequences of Action: Analysis

Seeing hope as action, then, is not so vague as it may sound at first. Not only have the kinds of action I speak of produced their specific traditions and concrete results, but they have also given us access to understanding what stands in the way of a dignified life for everyone. The other planes of my discussion need to be complemented by a Marxian one, so that we can speak of underlying socioeconomic structures, social systems of privilege and exploitation, indeed of ruling groups and classes. The attempts to create societies of greater human dignity have been opposed and will be opposed at every step by those who have something to lose by such attempts.

To keep up hope entails the effort of becoming clearer and clearer about what are the interests of exploitation and domination and oppression, about specifically what needs to be changed and specifically how. Sometimes it seems, however, that the clearer one becomes, the more formidable are the opponents, for all their fundamental moral weaknesses. Today, for example, sexual, racial, and class privilege continue to reign, and it often appears that the victories for human dignity are little more than tactical concessions granted by those in power. Their rule seems more subtle yet more stable for it; they sometimes seem to be able to weather any challenge, to co-opt, divide, and dishearten all movements for emancipation. Of course this seemed no less true in the past. The social and political systems overthrown by the French Revolution, the American Civil War, the Bolshevik Revolution, and the American Civil Rights Movement, seemed monstrous in their power as in their evil. But they fell, dramatically if only partially, in a series of historical upheavals that took on tidal force, even if today the transformations remain incomplete.

Keeping Hope

This sweeping world-historical picture may, however, give little comfort as we return to our original question about keeping alive the subjective attitude, hope. There may indeed be reasons to hope, but how, over the long years the struggle takes, which after all stretch well beyond one lifetime, can any given individual, can I, can you, keep up hope? It may well be that changes such as the end of apartheid will come "inevitably," but even so, it seems to be taking so tortuously long, to be so difficult, so painful, so costly. How can the will to act, can human hope, be sustained amidst times of exhaustion, discouragement, and defeat?

In reply, first, a sense of realism, of limits, is absolutely necessary for keeping hope. Hope worth the name is not a Pollyannish smile in the face of impending doom, but rather stems from the deepest possible appreciation of the weight of the world. It is grounded in a sense of tragedy. Hope is, above all, without illusion. It does not give false encouragement about how much can be changed or about how quickly. In this sense, grounded hope is the exact contrary of that optimism, that illusion of hope, which refuses to take the full measure of just how powerful is the South African state, or the inbred hierarchical values of class society, or the male identity-commitment to patriarchy. A hope determined to be without illusions maps the terrain of struggle painstakingly, even pessimistically. Only then can we know where lie the openings for what sorts of action, the fissures and fault lines to be exploited, the possible countertendencies. But where then lies the space for struggle, for example, in the face of the South African state's total offensive? What if there seem to be *no* openings? What is to be done in a time of retreat and fragmentation of the American women's movement or black movement? These questions are precisely the questions posed by an unflinching commitment to hope. They involve honoring the real-world basis of all pessimism.

But they do not entail, except for those who have been broken by them, abandoning the struggles for human dignity. Knowing fully the negative curves of the terrain to be covered is essential if hope is to be based on reality. After all, action does not mean just any action, as I said earlier, and indeed, not merely committed action charged with a sense of moral purpose. The point is to be as effective as possible within the constraints of the present situation. Indeed, test those borders, breach them if possible—but accept and work within them as necessary. In some situations this means regrouping, study, rethinking mistakes, recasting strategy and tactics—some of the current tasks of the liberation struggle in South Africa. In some situations, on the contrary, this means breaking through previously sacrosanct limits in order to make *the* revolution, in an unbounded sense of possibility. But at other times and places people pushed to the edge of their sense of humanity, with no space left to them for even imagining liberation, struggle mightily just to keep themselves from succumbing. As Victor Frankl describes them in *Man's Search for Meaning in the Modern World,* they achieve a phenomenal victory just to be able to arrange their few remaining belongings in a corner of a concentration-camp bunkhouse, to assert the barest human responses to the most anti-human degradation. The Warsaw ghetto fighters remind us again of how much, and how little, their situation allowed them: to die "for freedom and humanity." Limited to this narrowest of spaces, they stretched out to their full height and, in their utter failure, succeeded.

They acted from a complete appreciation of their situation. They knew that all they might do was temporarily stop the death machinery, perhaps avenge a few murders, and, above all, tell themselves, the Germans, and whoever might find out, that they *fought back.* Sometimes, such desperation, surprisingly, redefines the situation. But this does not make every situation an open one, allowing any possible response or outcome. Movements easily fall victim to the quasi-Leninist, quasi-Jacobin illusion that there are never really any defeats, only mistakes, that the "correct" strategy or the "proper" leadership would have produced victory. Nothing on earth, however, would have overthrown the South African state in 1984–86; nothing on earth would have brought full equality to American blacks in the 1960s, or to Western women in the 1970s. The "proper" leadership and "correct" strategy, if indeed they existed, would only have delayed the inevitable discouragement, fragmentation, and need to recover, regroup, and rethink.

What, then, becomes of hope during such inevitable hard times—today, for example? An American can learn much about hope in South Africa. Strange to say, in South Africa I do not at all find a mood of discouragement. The forces seeking fuller human rights in the United States are far more discouraged than are their comrades in the land of apartheid. In the current climate of repression, I have met no one who speaks about giving up. During my stay in South Africa it has become clear that those who kept hope are those who have learned to be both principled—to keep alive the feeling and ideas of love, shame, solidarity, and possibility with which they originally engaged themselves—and to be grounded in this world and its real prospects. Such people keep alive both vision and reality, and—above all—they accept the tension between them.

It is clear that one cannot keep up hope without keeping alive bedrock moral principles of solidarity, human caring, belief in human dignity and freedom. After all, these are and must remain the guiding principles, both the values to be fought for in the present and the anticipations of a better world. We must return to them again and again. We must share them between ourselves to remind ourselves of who we are and why we act. Keeping them alive must be one of our main impulses. We must recognize them when they are alive in history, in the world, in ourselves, and to do so we must count our victories. For example, even the changes in South Africa in the past fifteen years, however limited and few such victories are, are reasons to hope. They come from a movement's collective power, and it is important to experience that power at work in the most minor concession granted by the most grudging state. Moreover, it is important to sense that power as being part of a vast, collective *we* that stretches from this hall to the townships, from the past to the present; not only from Natal to the Cape but also to Harare and London and New York. As I myself have experienced, in the love and solidarity I have shared in South Africa, it stretches from Durban to Detroit. Anyone who has individually been part of the struggle may gain heart by learning to recognize the *we* that has produced victories elsewhere, and even to identify with it. It is especially important to do so during the inevitable dark moments.

At the same time, as I have suggested, keeping hope requires a schooling in realism. It is important to appreciate how little any one individual, or even a larger movement, can accomplish in any given moment. It is important to appreciate how significant an achievement it is even to convince a single person to think slightly differently. It must be understood how long it takes to build the kind of tidal force that creates basic social change. And how variegated the struggle must be; how, if we continue to speak metaphorically but realistically, a multiplicity of rivulets comes from the millions of individual droplets and form into rivers that alone form the tidal force that causes social change. In this respect, those who are active must beware of seeing a single right way in every situation. It is absurd to say, for example, that someone shouldn't teach or study engineering or business, but rather that he or she should act here or there, in this specific way. To keep hope, movements must learn the reality that in every struggle people inevitably will act along dozens of lines. Keeping hope requires learning to see the contribution that the dozens of lines make. Thus it requires avoiding becoming religious about "the" struggle. "The Movement" must be removed from quotation marks and capital letters and kept from becoming a force that drives its participants, alienating them from their purpose, from themselves, a joyless monstrosity, an exhausting force.

To keep hope, after all, requires a world-historical perspective that takes a long view. To keep hope is to be in it for the long haul. On a personal level this may suggest wanting to have children, to raise them, to marry them off, to have pleasures, love, fulfillments, and even personal successes—and to recognize that these are good in themselves as well as helping the struggle by making us more human. They keep people alert, whole, resilient, and perhaps even ultimately indomitable. Yes, people are suffering and, in South Africa, dying. And yes, we must constantly mourn our losses, our assassinated Rick Turners. But to preserve hope means to avoid letting that suffering, and the evil causing it, become principles of our own action. Keeping hope means learning to celebrate our victories as well as to mourn our defeats. Each celebration can join everyone who participates with that mighty movement of world history that we have been slowly, erratically, bringing into being.

Realism dictates understanding the alternation of victory and defeat, exhaustion and energy. History sometimes advances by moving one step forward, then two steps back. And sometimes by moving two steps forward and only one step back. Sometimes massive defeat is inevitable, and sometimes massive leaps forward are possible. It is necessary to learn how to recognize both victory and defeat. Those who cannot acknowledge and accept defeat, especially when the forces on the other side have more power, tend to turn defeats into disasters. Similarly, those who believe in liberation tomorrow have set themselves up for discouragement and a future of fear, apathy, and resentment.

I originally entitled these remarks "A Preface to Hope," but I find this language too imposing. In fact, it is only one of what should be thousands of such reflections taking place in the midst of the human project, reflections seeking to keep hope alive. It is a reflection meant as a consolation and a challenge, an invitation and an encouragement, coming from the United States to South Africa. And so I will end it as I began, paying homage to the spirit of Rick Turner. His spirit is indeed among all of us if we so choose, but his hope will be kept alive and fulfilled not only if we remember and honor Rick Turner, not only if we study his work—but if we use it in the way it cries out to be used, as guide, as inspiration, as a spur, and as a continued call to action.

Part Three

Reflecting

5

Ambiguities of White Rule

My favorite photograph from my trip to South Africa, taken on the day before I left the country, looks down from a high hilltop on the Cape. On the right is Pollsmoor Prison, on the left a wine estate cradled by the mountains. I stand there, almost dividing the two, wearing my new suede-cloth sport jacket, bought with the unused portion of my visiting lecturer's stipend. Token of white privilege, the jacket cost twice the average domestic worker's monthly wage. One enters the wine estate through high white gates, down an elegant drive, past older vineyards and older cramped housing for workers on the one side and spacious paddocks for horses on the other. The main house, converted to a restaurant, is being renovated after a fire. All the buildings, of Cape Dutch architecture, show meticulous care. The newest buildings are in a just-completed compound of model housing for workers which is kept off-limits to visitors. Beautiful and agriculturally progressive, the estate is one of roughly sixty thousand South African farms that depend for their prosperity on large numbers of resident (and nonunionized) black workers.

Just down the road is Pollsmoor Prison. A maximum security prison and then some, it is kept under extremely tight surveillance, with its walls capped by spirals of barbed wire. It is generally unremarkable, except perhaps for the fact of South Africa's extremely high prison population (a rate much higher than the prison population of the United States, as is its crime rate, as is its number of executions). At the time the photograph was taken, Nelson Mandela was incarcerated there. This fact made the prison one of the most magnetic places in South Africa. Removed from Robben Island because of the inspiring effect his presence was said to have on the other inmates, Mandela was brought here to the mainland. On the Island, at Pollsmoor, and more recently at a warden's house at Victor Verster Prison in Paarl, he is known to act towards his jailers, and to be treated by them, as the future president of South Africa.

To me the photograph suggests complexities, easily posed as opposites: the American observer becoming part of the picture of South Africa; the achievements of the white settlers (and their black laborers) alongside the white oppressive apparatus; the utter domination by whites over even the most authoritative of blacks; and yet, alongside the elegant world of white privilege, the unseen presence yet overwhelming moral authority of South Africa's black president-in-waiting.

I was rather surprised when I realized that I didn't show this slide in the first talks I gave on South Africa. Nor did I speak much about the positive effect some American and South African corporations are having in mixing whites and blacks at the workplace and giving a few blacks the opportunity for management positions. Nor did I dwell on the evident erosion of petty apartheid and even such major oppressions as influx control and the pass laws. And for months I didn't have a single conversation about certain problems that occupied me for whole days while I was in South Africa, such as tendencies within the United Democratic Front and the Congress movement towards authoritarian thinking and away from democracy.

Instead, without even thinking about it, I stayed with simpler shots, reflecting the less ambiguous story I told above in chapter 2: of galvanized metal shacks in KwaZulu in the Natal Midlands, tiny floorless prefabricated homes waiting for victims of the latest removals; of the outhouses that survived the destruction of Crossroads; of African women walking towards Nyanga Bush, carrying on their heads scrap construction wood for improving their illegal shanties; of District Six, once a thriving colored community sitting empty in the middle of Cape Town; of the checkpoint potentially barring the entrance to Glebelands Hostel near Durban; of the sole remaining building of the multiracial community once called Cato Manor, its decaying Hindu temple desolate against an empty ridge.

Upon returning home, at first I forgot all about the tensions of my favorite photograph, the endless conversations about what is likely to happen to South Africa, my own habitual reflections about the ambivalent role of white progress in the nonwhite world, and more than one fearful discussion about what majority rule might bring. I did not use tactical, political reasons to avoid the ambiguous and the contradictory, such as, for example, trying to drum up vigorous condemnation for apartheid. Rather, like the levels of my favorite photograph, the complexities, duly noted, became overpowered by the stunning moral simplicity of apartheid. But I always knew that I too would have to do what all of my friends in South Africa have long since learned to do: face the ambiguities. Inevitably, I began to confront the task of drawing my moral and emotional response to South Africa into a larger reflection that sifts through the various complexities and tensions I could not fail to notice.

Reforming Apartheid?

The first of these complexities was the absence of "blacks only" and "whites only" signs. A visitor looking for the most infamous humiliations of apartheid would have to look very hard indeed. As I mentioned in chapter 2, I saw only two explicitly racial signs, at a cemetery in the Natal midlands and at the Durban beaches. I myself saw blacks working in and patronizing restaurants, shops, groceries, and movie theaters. I saw black police directing traffic, black shop managers, black bank tellers. We were searched for terrorist devices by African security guards at the entrance to Durban shopping centers. If they do not quite mingle in downtown Durban, blacks and whites occupy the same space without incident. We were struck by an everyday, prosaic sight of blacks queuing up in downtown Durban at the various banks' automatic cash machines.

Opponents as well as advocates of apartheid impressed on me how much had changed in South African society over the past dozen or fifteen years, especially recently. Significantly enough, no one among the anti-apartheid South Africans I talked with dismissed the ending of these various forms of petty apartheid as meaningless. And they acknowledged that even some of the components of grand apartheid are being abolished. The infamous Immorality Act and Prohibition of Mixed Marriages Act have been scrapped. The abolition of the pass laws and of influx control, so long demanded, means that Africans may be able to move about freely in search of work and settle where they can in their group

areas, without dreading prosecution and expulsion. Job reservation for whites has been abolished, meaning that blacks will be
theoretically able to compete for any job until now statutorily reserved for whites. Trade unions may now legally bargain collectively. Anyone who doubts that these are major changes need only
consider the action in plays such as *Statements after an Arrest
under the Immorality Act* and *Sizwe Bansi is Dead;* their bitter
criticism of apartheid is based on situations that can no longer
happen.

Today, everyone agreed, compared with the time just before the
Soweto uprising over a dozen years ago, there are significantly
more middle-class blacks; far more blacks attend university, especially places like Natal and Wits; even if they do so uncertainly,
blacks move more freely, often shopping where they can afford to,
eating where they can afford to; they are building more middle-
class homes in the townships and are even moving into "gray
areas." And the black trade-union movement has become tolerated by capital and the state as a legitimate representative of workers' interests.

A first-time visitor may have difficulty making comparisons
with the past, but clearly these changes are more than window
dressing. For example, although we found central Durban oppressive and Mafikeng strange, the Market in Johannesburg felt very
much like an American city. Blacks and whites not only shared the
same space but interacted relatively easily, with no trace of subser-
vience or arrogance, eyes not averted from each other. On a Saturday we walked through shopping areas in downtown Johannesburg which had become almost totally occupied by blacks, who
come to shop from the townships. We saw a chess game in Joubert
Park between a black and a white man, watched intently by a
racially mixed crowd. And in Hillbrow, South Africa's most fa-
mous "gray area," blacks and whites work, shop, and live in the
same space.

To be sure, no one is quite sure how to take the new freedom of
movement. Half of African South Africa has already been excluded from much of this freedom by having been made citizens
of the "homelands." How long will they be permitted to move
freely, to build shantytowns or to rent in townships? Signs everywhere in Seapoint, Cape Town, declared that "we reserve the right
to refuse service." To whom, I wondered? Those "who are not

dressed to or do not behave to our standards" could be any black person as judged by a white proprietor, even if a smartly dressed black might hope to be served without incident.

A South African expatriate who visited recently was so struck by the changes in the fifteen years since he left that he decided to move back. A university teacher, he decided that he would be able to teach as never before: to black students, in a climate in which whites and blacks interact far more than when he left, and where political discourse has opened up remarkably. In spite of the repression, he thinks that South Africans speak, write, and think far more freely than before he left.

Such reforms are visible enough to have spurred the meteoric rise of the Conservative party, claiming allegiance to classical apartheid, to the place of official opposition. But these reforms are not enough to satisfy any of the blacks I met, or even to convince them that the government is sincerely trying to end apartheid. The state remains their enemy, the repressive tool of a minority that insists on holding onto the core of apartheid in and through all changes.

Blacks and white critics see the changes as concessions that have either been wrested from the state only after brutal struggles, or have been imposed by South Africa's white economic and political rulers in their own interests. The pass laws had become unenforceable, job reservation had made efficient labor management impossible, the signs of petty apartheid were ruining the country's image overseas. The leading conglomerate, Anglo-American Corporation, has come to acknowledge, like any modern capitalist enterprise, that labor unions have an unavoidable role to play in its future. Blacks welcome, but remain cynical about, all reforms as long as they do not eliminate the pillars of apartheid: the Population Registration Act, the Group Areas Act, and a constitution giving humiliating roles to Indians and "coloreds" and not even these shadows of power to Africans.

And they point out that the reforms occur in a police-state environment. This is reflected in an extended state of emergency, tens of thousands of detentions, prohibition of political meetings, closing of newspapers, assassinations of ANC leaders outside of South Africa and of anti-apartheid activists at home, and the banning of virtually all opposition activities. Not a single one of the reforms has addressed the fundamental question of South African society: white power over blacks. The ruling vision seems to be to remove area after area of statutory discrimination, while firmly leaving political, institutional, and structural power in the hands of whites. In other words, racial liberalization goes hand in hand with increased repression and undiluted white power.

Further changes are in the air. It may well be that group areas will be scrapped outright. And, reflecting expanding educational opportunities and the needs of a dynamic economy, it may well be that individual blacks will be allowed to rise, each according to his or her abilities. As black buying-power and skill-levels increase, a few blacks will move into high administrative positions, even commanding whites, and will live next door to whites.[1] It may be that a growing free-enterprise economy will slowly diminish the role of the state and of state corporations.[2] And local black "self-government" may allow individual blacks who accept these arrangements to achieve significant political roles on the national level, perhaps including major governmental positions. Or perhaps some more exotic scheme can be devised to remove the scandal of minority rule while avoiding the unacceptable: majority rule. This circle once squared, an end to employment discrimination, renewed economic expansion, unhindered free enterprise, and expanded black education will together create a South Africa which meets the aspirations of everyone. To facilitate this happy prospect, Clem Sunter, scenario planner for Anglo-American Corporation, calls for minimal sanctions, small government, decentralized power, and joint negotiation.[3]

This vision reveals how the liberal hopes of many whites who are willing to work and live alongside blacks of the same social class dovetail with the determination of enlightened Afrikaners to "adapt or die," as well as with the self-interest of South African capital. If, as I shall explore in the next sections, whites have been able to remake reality in South Africa as nowhere else, and have become accustomed to translating their wishful thinking into the real world, this vision is only the latest fantasy they would impose on black South Africa. It is a scheme for a sort of deracialized apartheid. If it were workable it would lead to an economic, social, and educational situation for blacks reminiscent of that in the United States, with allowances for the far greater inequality of today's South Africa. The "natural" workings of the economy, rather than the force of law, would ensure that the vast majority of blacks would remain in their group areas, attend woefully inferior schools, work at substantially lower wages and live on the margin, while a handful of them would be absorbed into the privileges of white society. The overt humiliations of apartheid would be largely scrapped, but its social, economic, and political substance would continue.

Blacks reject the offer. They see in it only continuing subjection to whites. A well-to-do Indian physician, living in a strikingly modern home, able to vote for the House of Delegates, which is a constitutional but virtually powerless and thoroughly compromised part of the apartheid government, expressed why. She spoke of what it was like to return to South Africa after vacationing or attending a medical conference overseas. She refuses to fly on South African Airways, so as not to support the state and to put off her return to the last possible moment. But in the queue of any airline, or on the flight itself, she senses the same phenomenon. "Men and women who, traveling overseas, were forced to be ordinary people, begin to grow in stature and self-confidence because they're going back to where they're special because they're *white*." She spits out this last word with all the rage of someone whose life has been spent on the other end of an arrogance that she can see reconstituting itself before her eyes. It is the arrogance, fundamentally, of those who hold power over others; this doctor clearly will never give in to it.

The white vision of reform, which reflects "a willingness to experiment, albeit on the most bizarre and contorted lines,"[4] remains an impossible dream. Its generosity, which may well be sincere, even though it is an economic and political necessity, is utterly contradicted by the determination to hold power. The new constitution provides eloquent testimony to this. One colleague sketched a genuine project of moderate constitutional change that might have been chosen in 1983 if the government had indeed wanted to slowly reform apartheid out of existence rather than entrench white hegemony: "a partial extension of the franchise to Indians and 'coloreds' within the old parliamentary system." This would have meant slowly including nonwhites in the institutions of effective power, rather than setting up dummy institutions for them and leaving all real power in white hands. "Had they followed the 'classical' Anglo-European model of franchise extension, the prospects for effective inclusion of excluded groups into a unitary system—and thereby both effectively (if piecemeal) democratizing the system and constraining the growth potential of the far right—would have been much better." Any decent intentions among the ruling whites are marred irrevocably by their insistence that *they* will be the ones who grant the changes that *they* decide, at a pace that *they* decide. And that the core of apartheid, white domination over blacks, continues as the condition of all reforms of apartheid. Even if the majority is allowed to live more humanly, the central color bar is intended to remain: the majority will not rule.

Irrationality

The depth of this determination makes all who are concerned about it dread the future of South Africa. It leads to one of the major questions preoccupying almost every South African I talked to: Can apartheid be ended without catastrophe? Granted that no ruling class gives up power gracefully before it has to, without a struggle, under what conditions is it thinkable for the rulers of South Africa to abolish the Population Registration Act, to accept the principle of one person, one vote in a unitary South Africa, and to negotiate towards majority rule and the end of a racial society? Will political, economic, and military pressure ever move them to end apartheid? Or are they incapable of being convinced, or defeated—short of being physically overthrown or destroyed?

Are they so wrapped up in racism, in their vision of white and Afrikaner identity, as to be unable to consider a more or less dignified surrender of political power? Perhaps they have come to so totally believe their own rhetoric about Afrikaner survival, or their own premises about white superiority and black inferiority, as to be unreachable. Then they will have gone off the deep end. They will have rendered themselves unable to find a way out of the laager.

If so, catastrophe lies ahead. Imprisoned in their own propaganda, white South Africans will live out the Afrikaner prophecy that the struggle to sustain apartheid poses only two alternatives, their survival or their destruction. They will continue to ignore what virtually everyone in South Africa seems to regard as "the inevitable." After holding onto power in ever more repressive, ever more violent ways, they will not stop at any brutality in what they have defined as their self-defense. They call to mind the American commander during the Tet offensive in Vietnam in January 1968, who destroyed the village of Ben Tre "in order to save it."

We know that it is irrational for them to destroy endlessly in order to save their power; or to refuse to accept the inevitability of black rule in a country which is overwhelmingly black; or to simply not accept black aspirations as being as valid as white. Those who rule South Africa, and their right-wing opposition, display a streak of domination so arrogant, so single-minded, so total, that in some fundamental ways it seems to deny reality. Still, this is nothing new in South Africa. On first impression we may also sense an irrationality about the system of racial classification itself, or in the ruthlessness with which apartheid was carried out, or in its abstract, designed character, or in the determination of those on the right of the government to reverse recent reforms and return to the past.

The point is that, even as one keeps making sense of South Africa, it keeps seeming *contrary* to sense. Certainly all understanding begins with the hard fact that apartheid has always been straightforwardly colonial: an unhypocritical, unashamedly direct and brutal system of racial domination. As many writers point out, the specifics of apartheid can be traced to specific class and ethnic interests of (mostly Afrikaner) labor, of (mostly Afrikaner) agriculture, of (English) mining capital, of nascent Afrikaner capital. Yet if it is obviously and undeniably a system of privilege, apartheid has an elusive quality as well—an obsessional, totalitarian character that seems independent of, or sometimes even contradictory to, what we normally think of as self-interest.

This characteristic is first of all something that a visitor can *sense,* something that seems contrary to reason or even to customary forms of oppression. For example, the visitor can glimpse the fruits of massive physical destruction launched after 1948 at places like Cato Manor, in Durban, visible from the porch of the visitor's flat at the University of Natal. Home to 125,000 Africans, Indians, and even a few whites, Cato Manor not only violated the Group Areas Act, but was difficult to control by the authorities. In the 1960s they removed every last resident and then tore it down. What I saw was only a vegetation-covered ridge at the center of which was the small white speck of a single surviving building, a desolate Hindu temple. A year later it, too, was destroyed. Perhaps it is the vast scope of the project, or its catastrophic fury, or its destruction of a complex human world in a bizarre ideological project: in all of these ways it seems contrary to sense.

To take a similar example, in the midst of densely populated Cape Town, District Six, a former "colored" community of 60,000 people, appears today as a green patch. One can study the history of each and every settled area destroyed since 1948,[5] and perhaps in each case grasp a specific reason for the destruction and resettlement. But their sum, still, boggles the mind. Between 1962 and 1980 3,522,900 people were removed.[6] Even after all the profits have been tallied, the new white homes accounted for, the ungovernable townships destroyed, and the political threat of blacks living near whites removed, we are still left to contemplate the astonishing: in a time of peace, one in six people was forcibly relocated by the South African state.

In a KwaZulu area in the Natal Midlands, as I mentioned above, I happened on a township-to-be, made up of neatly placed outhouses and galvanized metal one-room shacks with no floors. No one yet lived in this ghostly place. Perhaps it was waiting for the victims of other removals, waiting to become part of the story that includes Cato Manor and District Six, as well as Sophiatown and Crossroads. Certainly the specific intentions and detailed histories of each case are important, but the overall project, as described by a South African newspaper, adds up to "the most staggering example of social engineering attempted by any government since World War II."[7]

What specific forms of irrationality does it reflect? White arrogance? Racism? Fear? Afrikaner identity? One reason for talking about irrationality is that in carrying out and maintaining apartheid these drives seem to be moving on their own, rather than being functional adjuncts of a racial capitalism or of Afrikaner advance or of white economic or social privilege. A second reason is that those caught up in these drives are rendering themselves unable to return to reason. They are sawing off the plank permitting them to make their way back to calculations of costs and benefits—to negotiate with South Africa's future rulers guarantees for capital, minority rights, the length and features of a transition period, perhaps even protection of some jobs. Trapped in this laager of their own making, decisive segments of white South Africa may be becoming too blinded to be able to think: "Yes, we must face reality, we must safeguard our children's future and preserve as much of what we have built as is possible under majority rule."

But surely it is all a matter of self-interest. Those who live in, and study, South Africa have gotten used to it. Perhaps apartheid appeared irrational at one time, as it does to the first-time visitor, but, as a distribution of wealth and power, it is clearly explainable by self-interest. Apartheid can be seen as a ruthless form of social engineering shaped by specific material needs, whether of Afrikaners in general, of the South African capitalist system, of mine owners, of farmers and workers, or of Afrikaner capital dominating a coalition with the Afrikaner petty bourgeoisie and working class. In other words, designed and implemented "in order to . . . ," that is, to achieve specific and comprehensible material goals, apartheid is no more and no less than a functional and system-rational policy. Insofar as it is a matter of material self-interest, apartheid consists of specific forms of economic accumulation, of political power, of social and political privilege.[8] Opposition strategies may accordingly try to raise the cost of retaining those structures in their present form, to the point where key members of an ultimately rational, because self-interested, leadership will decide they are no longer worth maintaining. For example, we may ask, how much did it cost to hold onto white rule in Rhodesia? As civil war wore on, the rhetoric faded before the reality, and whites yielded power. Even if the privilege-softened human mind avoids facing reality, pain is a great educator. In time, loss of life, international isolation, and, ultimately, economic boycott, became too much for white Rhodesians to bear.

This is the hardheaded "self-interest" model that was argued while I was at the University of Natal by Professor Masipula Sithole of the University of Zimbabwe. Beyond it lies the grim possibility I am suggesting, that far more irrational dynamics are also at work in South Africa today.[9] Obviously there is no simple litmus test that can tell us in a foolproof way when we are confronting an irrational policy, an extremely irrational one verging on madness, and one that is clearly mad. Elsewhere I have explored the far end of the continuum, some of the most extreme cases of our century, situations which even as they may have served self-interest became so irrational as to perhaps warrant use of the term "mad." Nazi Germany's attack on the Jews was a sustained and deep-seated paroxysm of social madness, because in it the Nazis radically ruptured with reality in regarding, redefining, and treating the Jewish people as subhumans deserving to be exterminated. Under Stalin, the leadership of the Soviet Union, subjected to overwhelming pressures, tried to do the impossible by industrializing overnight and building socialism in an isolated, underdeveloped, peasant society.[10] To the degree that apartheid resembles these or other grotesque situations of our century, the calculations of "stepping up the cost" and "self-interest" need to be mixed with an urgency about how to avoid disaster. After all, in our century societies have again and again given themselves over to systematic and massive assaults on reality, becoming organized now according to deranged perceptions (of enemies, for example), now according to deranged intentions (of creating or upholding the impossible, for example).[11]

In this century, over one hundred million people have been killed, often as a result of such breaks with reality. True, all of the genocidal projects have been done for vital social reasons. And they have all contained their coldly rational components (for example using the latest in scientific techniques), and have often unfolded without so much as a word of rage, as in the absurd and futile American effort to transform South Vietnam into an "independent non-Communist" society. But cold or hot, defending against enemies or destroying "subhumans," and above all, no matter how coolly rational they may appear, such projects have again and again led to catastrophe. Sometimes the catastrophe is the victim's alone; sometimes it even destroys what it is trying to save. Is South Africa heading in a similar direction? And if so, why?

This question recurs every time the state bans a newspaper or individual or organization, every time its repressive net tightens or another terrorist attack is carried out against anti-apartheid activists such as Dulcie September or Albie Sachs or David Webster. "Yes," white South Africa seems to say, "we may adjust apartheid to circumstances, but only at a pace we shall decide, and above all by retaining total control over the society. Under no conditions will we give up our power."[12] This determination to hold on to power in spite of everything violates a most basic premise of any rationality—that human intentions and actions must fundamentally conform to, and ultimately yield to, the broad limits imposed by human and natural reality.

Against the Grain of History?

No wonder. From the beginning, whites have seemed able to transform the land and its people virtually at will, according to their own vision. Apartheid was only the most recent plan to designate and reshape Africans, against their wishes, as the whites' own "hewers of wood and drawers of water," as well as to carve out distinct inferior classifications for Indians and those of mixed race. In this sense the system is the child of the Western power that was imposed from the beginning with an almost godly arrogance.

Still, the recent project of apartheid must be compared with the enslavement of millions of Africans from the seventeenth to the nineteenth century. The reason why apartheid appears less rational than slavery lies in the distance of three hundred years. In other words, any claims about reality and irrationality inevitably rest on historical ground. What "makes sense" or is possible in one period does not do so, is not possible, in another. Over the centuries several realities changed beyond recognition—not only social, political, and technical realities, but also ethical and psychological ones. By 1948, for example, the general human sense of basic rights, democracy, and equality had grown enormously, to the point of invalidating racist thought and making brute racial oppression less morally and politically thinkable. Human social progress, through struggle and its resulting institutional and moral incarnations, had little by little expanded the prevailing sense of what it meant to be human. By the end of World War II, the current view of universal human dignity was coming to entail, among other things, universal political rights and national self-determination.

Against this grain of history, the new political rulers of South Africa elaborated a social order imposing a more tightly controlled servile status on millions of people—in the middle of this century of self-determination. As the rest of Africa was achieving its political independence, South African blacks were being subjected to total colonial control and shaped, from the outside and against their will, as no more and no less than a movable, manipulable pool of cheap labor.

What, to return to the question, is the irrationality of apartheid? We have enough hindsight to know that it succeeded in making its apparent irrationality into a social system; and enough hindsight, equally, to know that the project was ultimately doomed. Even if it could be implemented and made to seem just another nasty social system, no more or less irrational than any other, it was equally bound to be resisted, with a force that would only grow in strength over the years. No people would fully and finally yield to it, and in the end they will permanently war against it until it is overthrown. They will ultimately expose apartheid for what it is, a violation of sense, an effort to do the impossible.

The violation lies in going against historically attained human reality. In strengthening and systematizing a racial hierarchy when similar hierarchies were everywhere being overcome, apartheid was an unbridled assertion of power over humans in a world where humans have been bringing that kind of power under limits. The irrationality lies in the imposition of a system of total social engineering, a sort of science-fiction plan which designs another people's lives, at a time when everywhere else people have been winning the right to control major features of their own lives. The rupture with reality lies in the systematic, deliberate attack on the human essence in a world whose main struggles have increased human dignity.

In South Africa this meant, not so coincidentally,[13] denying the humanity of those very Africans who during the 1940s had more and more been laboring alongside whites, been moving physically closer to whites, whose clothes and habits were becoming more and more like those of whites, who had just mounted a major bus boycott and squatters' movement involving tens of thousands of people, and who had just risen up in a dramatic mine-workers' strike—in short, those who were proving their claim to full humanity day after day, in ways it would have been difficult to ignore. Apartheid tried systematically to deny, and to reshape according to a new, externally imposed scheme, the reality of black South Africans.[14]

If apartheid went against the grain of history, and in this sense may be judged irrational, it was certainly not an essential break with the reality of the lives black people had been forced to live before 1948. Pass laws were already well established, as were the farm-labor and migrant-labor system and the system of tribal reserves. For years the African population had been systematically "underdeveloped" for whites, all the more rapidly and systematically since the discovery of diamonds and gold during the last half of the nineteenth century. Despite fierce struggles, the colonial project had already been successfully imposed. In other words, the world-historical process of European domination over the nonwhite rest of the world was already solidly established in South Africa, perhaps more profoundly so than elsewhere because of its mineral wealth, temperate climatic zones, and the consequent large white population. Apartheid did not invent, but it solidified, codified, and systematized all of this.

But if what was done after 1948 only built on what had happened before, and was different "only" in its scope, its system, and its conscious and deliberate spirit, it completed a massive physical transformation of black South Africa. It is important to grasp the full impact of what blacks experienced as a single white project from 1652 to 1948 and after: from a free people living on their land, however meagerly and humbly by Western standards, Africans were herded into white history as the residents of one vast labor and concentration camp. It is as if not only their land but their very being was redefined, by the Europeans, for the Europeans. It was as if their very reality as human beings was systematically attacked and transformed, according to some kind of demented imperial vision.

Sources

Demented? What does the qualification add to our understanding? Its purpose is to underscore that the entire project, from conquest to expropriation to proletarianization to apartheid, is as grotesque an assault on human reality as history has ever seen. And that it is equally one of the world's great acts of denial. Yet as I have emphasized, even if apartheid was, and remains, in some sense deeply irrational, material self-interest has also been served by it. "Ethnic mobilization" created a significant economic advance for most Afrikaners, and English and Afrikaans capital alike flourished after the Nationalist victory.[15] Black industrial labor, which had been becoming organized and militant, was reduced to passive acquiescence under the new order, the migrant system so vital to mining capital was stabilized, agricultural workers were once again tied to their farms. Hundreds of thousands of Afrikaners were employed by the state and the burgeoning parastatal (public and semipublic) economic sector. White workers, who had seen a decline in their wages relative to Africans for the first time in history during World War II, sought and won renewed protection. To stabilize this new set of arrangements, any potential long-term political threat from an increasingly articulate and spirited black movement was to be liquidated once and for all by physically remaking the political, social, and residential map of South Africa, beginning with statutory classification according to the Population Registration Act.

On the one hand, then, it seems as if each detail of the project can be explained in terms of such historical and class roots. On the other, it was a total and systematic violation of the human essence which went against the grain of history, and, as we now see, of possibility. What are the social sources of such a stupendous ambition? Why, at this specific time and place, did specific social groups concoct, and carry out, such an extraordinary, and, we now know, ultimately unworkable scheme?

How do we explain the fervor and conviction that were needed to plan and carry out a system of total racial domination? Broadly speaking, I have referred to two kinds of explanations of apartheid: the first lays it at the door of capitalism, the second at the door of the Afrikaner people. The first makes it not at all irrational but quite functional, a system of "racial capitalism"; the second may equally make it a functional aspect of the Afrikaner advance but also pays attention to factors that are more ideological, and less materially grounded, such as Afrikaner mythology or religion or, more generally, identity.

To my mind neither set of explanations gets to the irrational source of apartheid. Neither does Lipton's emphasis on the role of workers and constant stress on self-interest, nor Dan O'Meara's study of the creation of Afrikaner nationalism, even though each of these adds a vital element to the discussion. The insights of *Capitalism and Apartheid* and *Volkskapitalisme* suggest that what we usually think of as social and political strength is not at the source of apartheid. One root of apartheid, I would argue, following their suggestions, lies rather in an elemental social weakness. If power and political will were required to carry out apartheid, so was weakness, social and moral weakness. Power, will, and weakness: these take shape and cohere in a crisis, characterized by a trauma and a process of social dysfunction.

First, to repeat, apartheid is rooted in the world-historical reality of white power over blacks, which gives rise to the supreme arrogance of almost every facet of white relations with blacks. And, second, it is also rooted in the ways in which white expropriation of the country combined with capital's priorities to create blacks as the whites wished them to be: the migrant labor system, the native reserves, and the system tying agricultural labor to farms. But, third, apartheid is also a project of the defeated: those once-Boers who, vanquished militarily by British arms at the turn of the century and then uprooted from the countryside and massively impoverished by the development of English-speaking capital, responded by creating themselves into a *volk* in the 1930s and 1940s.

The project of creating an Afrikaner nation was fueled by several features of their situation. They were dispossessed and impoverished to such an extent that 30 percent were classified as "poor whites" in 1932; all Afrikaners were treated as second-class citizens by the English; the destruction of rural society wrecked the social soil of the Afrikaner petty bourgeoisie; and aspiring Afrikaner capitalists developed the determination to pull themselves up by the bootstraps of the *volk*.[16] Why did these economically and socially oppressed people not unite with English workers or Africans against the larger economic forces (and dominant social class, namely, the English bourgeoisie) that were overwhelming them? Massive numbers of white workers had come to South Africa, but all had done so within the framework of the European project: to wrest the land from Africans and exploit it and them for the benefit of the Europeans. Making common cause with other whites in the expropriation and impoverishment of Africans, from the beginning they ruled out any class-based labor strategy. Thus even had Boer workers wished to do so—and they did not— the racist as well as English-dominated character of working-class organizations ruled out any effective class unity. When large numbers of Africans became urbanized and proletarianized, particularly during World War II, and when they showed a capacity for concerted resistance, by then it was already too late. By then they were perceived as a threat by other workers, not a possible ally.

As H. J. and R. E. Simons say, "White Laborism has been a

primary cause of policies that incite racial hostility, isolate color groups, and dissolve class consciousness in color consciousness. The British immigrants who founded the Transvaal labor movement early in the century aspired to mastery over the African." [17] The unanticipated result of this pursuit of racial privilege was a crippled, corrupt labor movement unable to confront capital on its own. As Lipton points out, white labor's decisive struggle against capital, in the 1920s, was to make the job color-bar prevail, a bar that successfully reserved skilled work for whites at artificially high "civilized" rates. "White workers won, not because of their industrial power—which was unable to prevail against the Chamber [of Mines]—but because of their political power." [18]

Labor lacked industrial power because it was fatally split into its three components: the skilled English, the less-skilled Afrikaans, and the far-lower-paid blacks. And between the wars no other social force, especially English-speaking capital, was strong enough to assert its rule. In other words, during this period South Africa suffered from a crisis of hegemony. This crisis was rooted in the class dynamics of a capitalist society, hierarchically split into two ethnic groups, which was still deeply imbedded in the colonial project. During the years of economic and political crisis leading up to 1948, no class or social force was able to impose its will on the society.

The Afrikaner coalition that finally filled this void was the creation of a deliberate project. In a sense, Boers consciously shaped themselves into Afrikaners during the years after the defeat at the hands of the British. They acted out of a combination of weakness and power. For all their "anti-imperialism" and even "anti-capitalism," the coalition of workers, petty bourgeoisie, farmers, and nascent capitalists that created itself as the Afrikaner *volk* had no intention or ability to actually challenge the economic dominance of English capital. Even as they decided to sever ties with Britain, they accepted working within the dominant class and economic framework. [19] Like all right-wing "people's" revolts, the Afrikaner *volk* scarcely touched the structure of capitalism. Rather, they sought entry into it.

This unstable coalition, functioning within the capitalist framework, suffered from a fundamental weakness: it lacked *social* power. It was neither a united labor movement nor the owner of industry. It took over political power and passionately launched the only two sets of projects that were possible to it and that could hold it together. The first was to create apartheid; the second was to use the state to develop specifically Afrikaner social and economic power *alongside* that of the English. Whatever other interests apartheid served (such as the interest of English mining capital), it was an Afrikaner goal. It was an extreme, ideological project which, even as it had its economic reasons, could be hatched and carried out only by a coalition trapped in a mixture of social and economic weakness and racial arrogance, a coalition that deeply believed, and acted on, its extreme vision of supremacy.

The dynamics leading to apartheid, I am suggesting, are distorted ones. They stem from a situation blocked from the beginning, in which the dominant economic power, English capital, was no longer able to assert itself as the dominant political power, but in which workers were unable to organize effectively as workers. Thus the different Afrikaner groups found themselves able to gain political power by doing the only possible thing they could to advance themselves without directly challenging capital, namely, be drawn together *as* Afrikaners. It is worth constantly stressing the strange, twisted product that this situation of structural weakness and defeat produced: the overweening will to wholly determine other lives, in every major aspect and from beginning to end, to treat them fundamentally as subservient laborers who must be controlled at every step.

I sketch these lines of explanation not to settle the question about the sources of apartheid but to stress why no single answer I have encountered seems adequate to the phenomenon, because of the interpenetration in South Africa of race and class, of ideology and system, of ethnicity and interest, of rational and irrational, and above all, of impotence and power. The horrible, unstable, yet totalitarian aspect of South African life stems not from the maturity and self-confidence of any social force, be it capital or the Afrikaner *volk*. Rather, it stems from a dynamic similar to those which have produced other twentieth-century catastrophes, an explosive tension caused by the fundamental social weakness of those wielding state power. Above all, I would suggest, it is wrong to see today's apparently all-powerful apartheid state as reflecting great social self-confidence, for this ignores the intense weakness and profound sense of siege that led to the creation and consolidation of Afrikaner identity and its concomitant, apartheid. And, I would argue, this weakness continues today in spite of both the Afrikaner social and economic advance and the enormous power of the South African state.

Social weakness and racial domination; political power without social power; impotence in power. Perhaps these contradictions give a sense of the strain at the root of "solutions" like apartheid. They help explain the contradiction that can be seen constantly in the South African state: the self-pitying rhetoric we hear from its leaders as they act with crushing power. Are those who seem addicted to total control adrift in a situation out of their control? We may want to take heart from the fundamental instability conveyed in this contradiction, knowing that a resolution is "inevitable." But what kind of resolution?

Where Will It End?

I asked above whether apartheid might be ended without catastrophe. Has white South Africa become unreachable by any politics short of total war? Has it gone off the deep end? I also cited a Zimbabwean colleague's optimistic comparison with Rhodesia. Is it likely to work out this way? Or is there something so irrational about the situation that we have to abandon any hope of hardheaded self-interest carrying the day? Much of history, and especially of twentieth-century history, gives us reason to despair about such hopes winning out. Certainly, I hope that the irrationality I have been exploring will yield to the hard rationality of struggle: calculations of possibility, reality, interest, and, ultimately, survival.

However, it should be clear that both strands are present in South Africa, the rational and the irrational. Both have deep historical and structural roots. Today they arrange themselves across the political spectrum. The white minority is clearly split. The ruling powers, today supported by a majority of English speakers, want to reform aspects of apartheid while preserving white rule. The state bureaucracy, supported by masses of Afrikaans- and English-speaking whites and sections of the Afrikaner and the English bourgeoisie, seem totally unbending on the decisive issue of power. They seek to create the impossible: apartheid by consent, imposed by force. They are trying feverishly to square the circle, making changes while tightening their grip on the state's repressive apparatus. To their right, growing numbers of whites are suffering under what is becoming a permanent economic crisis, or fear the loss of jobs and privileges when the majority lays claim to the state. Or simply cannot tolerate even the limited and controlled forms of black-white integration the reformist state seems bent on carrying out. They want to reject all compromise—for material as well as ideological reasons—and claim that they will retreat to the laager and fight to the finish. My analysis of irrationality would make me not doubt their convictions or their courage, or indeed their genocidal and suicidal determination. Insofar as their jobs and petty privileges are tied to apartheid, they also have the most to lose when the majority lays claim to the state. And then there are those who are openly against apartheid, "but—." They are not unequivocally in favor of majority rule. Now they cooperate with the state's demand for military production, and now they meet with the ANC to discuss the future. Now they finance certain anti-apartheid activities like schools, newspapers, and theaters, and now they applaud the state president for controlling disorder. Now they oppose group areas and seek to rebuild District Six as an open area, and now they remain silent on the single decisive issue of majority rule. When majority rule comes, without their help and in spite of their resistance, they will claim to have supported it discreetly all along, and will seek to establish their place in the sun in a new South Africa. Then there are those whites who, seeing and accepting the reality that they are a minority in South Africa and that blacks will rule or everyone's lives and interests will be ruined, are by conviction or pragmatism willing to live under majority rule. Finally, there are those who have been courageously acting on behalf of a nonracial South Africa, out of conviction.

Politically, beneath these layers of whites are "coloreds" and Indians, never as totally oppressed as Africans, but never the equal of whites. Rather than decisively seeking to make them their allies, whites treated, and continue to treat, them as blacks, disenfranchising and humiliating them. Even if with ambivalence, they have become part of the repressed majority. That majority continues to percolate, agitate, and, occasionally, to erupt. After Sharpeville, the second explosion took sixteen years; after Soweto, the third took eight. The summer of 1989 saw the beginning of a new campaign of defiance. When will the next explosion take place? And what form will it take? When, if ever, will realistic strategic calculation prevail among whites? Or will hysteria and siege mentality win out? Will Sithole be proven right, or will the irrational streak dominate, perhaps to the point of madness, bringing down the whole society? This question, finally, cannot be answered by any analysis. We may have a sense of the elements in play, but their relative strength is not yet decided. It would be impossible to forecast how they will turn out, but it is not impossible to work to make them turn out in the best possible way for all concerned. The answer will emerge in the struggle itself.

6

Ambiguities of the Struggle

How, then, will apartheid be overthrown? In these reflections on its ambiguities, let me stress that I do not consider the question of violence to be one of them. To my ears, Oliver Tambo answered this question definitively when he appeared on Canadian television in early 1987. Pressed by his interviewer on ANC violence against the South African state, Tambo refused to be placed on the defensive, but instead slowly drew together his considerable moral force and dignity. He answered, deliberately and simply: "We have no alternative." And then he paused for several seconds and looked at his interviewer challengingly before continuing, leaving a space in which the full meaning of his words could reverberate. The silence was as eloquent as his words.

It said: If we had an alternative, we certainly would use it, because we have not taken the decision lightly. But we have tried every other means, and each of them has been declared illegal by a regime that denies our people's fundamental human rights. What would you do if you were in our place? Can you who are not oppressed really dare to moralize about what we, who do not even have your help, must do in order to free ourselves?

But Tambo certainly did not mean that the South African state will be overthrown by violence. The role of violence in the ANC's strategy has been limited: to continue a campaign of armed propaganda in order to remind both the state and its supporters on the one side, and the masses supporting the ANC on the other, that it is a potent force. Its main actions are political: efforts to gain support for sanctions and increased legitimacy overseas, and steps to move towards negotiations with the South African government.[1]

The ANC does not engage in all-out guerrilla war for several reasons. First, because the South African state is so politically and militarily powerful, and so tightly controls the country as well as paths to and from it, that a sustained campaign of guerrilla war is simply not possible at the present time. The state's networks of informers, its complete mastery of the technical means at its disposal, its power to strike quickly, its ability to attack beyond the border of South Africa, its willingness to launch massive reprisals—all militate against mounting a serious violent struggle. At the same time, the ANC seems restrained by its own traditions. It has historically been committed to nonviolence. This is shown in its determination, very unlike the behavior of so many of the world's colonialist masters, to *not* destroy the country in order to save it. It is worth stressing that whites in general have not been its target, nor does it aim at a radical social transformation beyond abolishing apartheid. As its many critics within the liberation struggle point out, the ANC/UDF movement, which takes the Freedom Charter as its touchstone, is committed to a respectable, moderate, and universalist vision—a middle-class vision of a nonracial South Africa governed by a broad coalition of social forces. Organizations within the other major opposition grouping, the National Forum, on the contrary, stress the need for class organization and working-class leadership, excluding whites from any significant position within the movement, and the need to struggle for black liberation from racial capitalism. Whether one agrees or disagrees with the Congress movement's strategy (I will discuss this further below), there is no doubt that it has been amazingly effective in creating a worldwide anti-apartheid coalition.

In the eyes of all those with eyes to see, the patent evil of apartheid and the state's brutal use of its power combines with the ANC's restraint and middle-class universalism to produce a set of moral realities. On the one hand, apartheid is regarded as evil by every standard of human rights in the world today, leaving the South African state without recourse to any positive human value.[2] On the other hand, the ANC's appeal to what are considered to be the most basic universal values gives it a compelling moral dignity. Essentially nonviolent, the South African liberation movement asks no more than people everywhere else have already won for themselves and enshrined in their constitutions. For people outside of South Africa, the opportunity to support such a noble movement against such an evil system makes South African liberation the great moral cause of the last quarter of the twentieth century. Hundreds of thousands of activists all over the world have been drawn into one of the great rarities, a campaign to remove an evil without doing or supporting evil.

The Question of Sanctions

Thus the appeal of sanctions and divestment. The support movement denounces the web of complicity and makes the case for rupturing with it. Behaving morally becomes an overwhelming argument to break with evil. The American Friends Service Committee's study, *South Africa: Challenge and Hope,* presents this concisely:

> Involvement in apartheid is a continuum of complicity. At the worst end of the continuum is total support for apartheid; at the other end is total rejection of any benefit from it. The sale of stock profiting one from business in South Africa is clearly a movement away from involvement in apartheid and toward freedom from it.[3]

A notion of responsibility and complicity similar to that which I presented in chapter 3 is combined with an insistence on "freedom from" apartheid, as if it is those in the United States who need to be liberated. A political act is called for that is above all a moral act.

The strategic role of sanctions becomes evident after a moment's reflection on the current ineffectiveness of the strategy of "fighting and negotiating." Not only will the state not negotiate, but the ANC is not really free to or able to fight under current political and military conditions. Thus the ANC has engaged in a long-term diplomatic offensive, alongside its armed struggle, to gain recognition and to win major sanctions against South Africa as a way of crippling the state so that it will enter into negotiations. Yet through the 1980s sanctions have run into a brick wall—namely, the Reagans, the Thatchers, and other hypocritical wielders of state power who declaim against violence while subsidizing terrorism, threatening nuclear war, and fighting conventional wars.[4] Moreover, in supporting UNITA, the United States openly aligned itself with the South African state against Angolans and Namibians, and also against the majority of South Africa. Outrageously, the Reagans and Thatchers have played to the hilt their self-assigned role, of moral judge of the Oliver Tambos! They successfully fought off the kind of concerted and total sanctions which alone might have any hope of shaking the South African state.

No negotiations, no effective armed struggle, no meaningful sanctions—against such obstacles, the path to liberation will be a complex and contradictory one, and threatens to stretch out ahead for many years. Perhaps this is why a number of sophisticated and radical white South Africans surprised me by expressing their discomfort about divestment. Their anti-apartheid convictions and activities were beyond question, but even Marxists among them pointed to certain positive actions of capital, and specifically mentioned the effects of American businesses operating under the Sullivan principles. When divestment takes place and South Africans buy up the firms, as more than one proponent of this long-term progressive perspective pointed out, the reforms often go out the window.

An Afrikaner woman I spoke with made no secret of her racism: blacks "are biologically inferior." Yet she also seemed to reflect the positive consequences of the Sullivan principles. Working for an American company, for the first time in her life she had encountered blacks as other than servants and inferiors. Helped by race relations seminars at the workplace, she has begun to see, and treat them, as equals. A mass of contradictions, she refers to school biology texts "proving" racial inferiority, considers the ANC but not the South African state to be violent, and worries about being discriminated against in the future. But she also points to how much her own generation has already changed, feels that majority rule is inevitable, and most of all asks for enough time to become accustomed to the idea.

I confess that this discussion made me feel less than righteous about the issue of divestment. Isn't it important that some whites, by working side by side with blacks, learn to accept them as equals? Considering how few blacks have been allowed to develop political and administrative skills under apartheid, won't it take many years before black skills and confidence have been built up to the point where they can make a real transition possible? In other words, mustn't apartheid be broken down in thousands of practical and personal ways along with being attacked politically?

This long-term progressive perspective argues that majority rule will not be won today or tomorrow. It will be demanded, and people will die for it, but blacks are not yet strong enough inside South Africa, nor do they have enough support outside of South Africa, to force the state to throw in the towel. Nor do whites feel sufficiently demoralized, or isolated, to feel they have to yield power. The end of apartheid is "inevitable," everyone knows it, but it is not impending. If this is true, I heard more than once, it will be necessary to take the time to build black skills and confidence and strength, until the majority's force becomes truly irresistible. And, at the same time, it will be necessary to foster the interactions that will break down white intransigence and encourage white acceptance.

A related analysis of sanctions focuses on the way in which the current economic crisis makes increased repression inevitable by driving poor whites to the right. The spectacular rise of the Conservative party is fed, in equal doses, by concessions to blacks and by the worsening economic situation. The state becomes more repressive in order to keep the political support of these ever-more-rabid whites, even as it cannot offer to relieve their economic distress through an expanding economy. As one colleague said, "They cannot stem the drift of whites to the extreme right without substantial economic growth, and they cannot secure economic growth without the serious political reconstruction that the growth of the extreme right-wing movement renders impossible. If there is a single good argument against sanctions, this is it."

The only problem is that the state shares these arguments, out of its own insistence on keeping political power in white hands. And so do the major corporations, out of their insistence on keeping their hold over economic power. The state is carrying out widespread repression as it seeks to modify, but retain, apartheid, and is seen *only* as an enemy by most blacks. The businesses were responsible for and profited from many of the original apartheid institutions, such as the pass and hostel systems, but they have recently criticized some, but not all of, the system that most blacks identify as apartheid. When capital speaks of an expanding economy undermining apartheid, it is clearly mouthing its own self-interest, which in this respect is the same as the state's. But can blacks be convinced that what is good for Anglo-American Corporation is also what is good for South Africa? Blacks remember decades of economic expansion which only solidified apartheid;

when Anglo-American speaks of sanctions harming blacks, blacks reply by arguing *for* being harmed—in order to hasten the change they regard as decisive, the coming of majority rule.[5]

In other words, they tend to regard these gains, such as the contradictory yet dawning acceptance of blacks by the woman I spoke with, as being too little and too late to make a difference. They do not want to wait until they are considered "ready" by someone else. They feel ready now. Even if it is analytically correct, the long-term progressive perspective amounts to whites telling blacks to wait. The only thing that will force them to wait is continued repression. Once again, the real issue is power. If we accept that South Africa's white political and economic rulers will or should steer the society for the foreseeable future, our concern should be to convince them to ameliorate the living conditions of blacks. Then, it would stand to reason, one should be "realistic" and seek out various forms of "constructive engagement" to convince, badger, and help them to do so. Above all, we should do nothing that would anger the state, or weaken the control over the state or the economy of those who seek change.

Blacks reject this perspective because it is saturated with the premises of white minority rule. Every black I spoke with, with the exception of a single civil servant in KwaZulu, demanded complete and total sanctions (the sole exception seemed caught between her own feelings and the Inkatha party line; she called for "more pressure, but not sanctions"). The political conflict has gotten to the point where blacks are begging for the outside world to bring white South Africa to its knees as the only way to bring it to its senses.

As the stalemate continues, and as the repression inside South Africa continues, the pressure will grow on the ANC to escalate attacks. Yet asking its foreign supporters to accept a full-scale guerrilla war against the South African state will mean asking them to accept its doing evil in order to do good. This is precisely the difficult path traced by the plays of Sartre I mentioned in the introduction: from the insistence on clean hands, leading to catastrophe, to the acceptance of dirty hands. I earlier approvingly cited Sartre's efforts to create a dialectical morality (especially as one of the supports for my own decision to go to South Africa in the first place; a visitor cannot hope for "freedom from," but rather must openly risk "involvement in," apartheid). I suggested that the approach seeking clean hands is naive. Sartre would add that it is easily disillusioned and ignores the pervasiveness of violence in social life.[6]

Ultimately, unless American and British policy changes drastically—to the point not only of these great powers imposing severe sanctions themselves but insisting that countries like Switzerland, Israel, Japan, and Taiwan cut ties with South Africa, and perhaps of recognizing the ANC and breaking relations with Pretoria—the ANC, blacks within South Africa, their internal political organizations, and the anti-apartheid support movement overseas will have to prepare for the trauma of an extended civil war. It is worth remembering that sanctions were effective in Rhodesia because they were far-reaching *and* accompanied by a civil war. Blacks within South Africa have already been living through a civil war since 1984; for them it will only mean an escalation. For the anti-apartheid movement outside the country it will be difficult, however, to accept the destruction of the clear-cut moral appeal that has made possible the massive worldwide campaign for divestment and sanctions. A genuine guerrilla war will traumatize many of those who oppose apartheid, because of its patent insistence that liberation cannot come without doing enough harm to make the whites surrender power. In the process, the democratic movement of South Africa will lose its halo, and the country will become like the other tormented places of the world, torn between competing and confusing claims of good and evil.

Tribal Conflict?

We can expect an escalation of three kinds of violence: between blacks and whites, between anti-apartheid blacks and supporters of Chief Gatsha Buthelezi, and among blacks within the movement for liberation. The best-known and most deadly struggle between blacks is the "black-on-black" violence between UDF supporters and members of Buthelezi's Inkatha movement. Many defenders of minority rule point to it. After all, they say, if Africans so hate each other, a third party has to keep order for everyone's self-protection. As the violence has increased in Natal since my visit, I can only suspect that this kind of verbal nonsense has increased.

Surely the violence is one of apartheid's great recent successes. Although Chief Buthelezi is both brilliant and complex, he is regarded with hatred and fear by most anti-apartheid activists I met, white and black. They point out that his hostility to apartheid does not keep him from being kept in power by the apartheid state; that his commitment to "free enterprise" does not keep him from running a patronage system that would rival the state's if he had the resources; that his profession of nonviolence towards whites does not keep his supporters from murdering black opponents in the Natal townships he controls. At least three factors are at work in the tension: the state-sponsored revival of tribalism since 1948, encouraging atavistic loyalties and hostilities; the creation of privileged groups of blacks, allied to the state, who stand to be threatened by any spread of UDF support and, even more, by majority rule; and the state's tolerance—some say encouragement—of such conflict. These factors revolve around the state's desire to keep Africans at bay by giving power over them to traditional tribal chiefs.

In Bophuthatswana we met Credo Mutwa, a well-known Zulu widely suspected of working for the state, who had come to construct a model Tswana village as a museum. "A people who forgets its past is lost," he told us after a brilliant stream of hype designed to dazzle Americans. And in Bop we also heard about how non-Tswanas were having their scholarships revoked at Unibo. And about how our hosts were doing battle with the appropriate government agency trying to get a residence permit for their non-Tswana housekeeper—so she could build a home in Mmbatho instead of being forced to return home to "her" bantustan. All of this reflects a deliberate policy, carried out by whites and blacks, of tribal regression.

Life in the bantustans shows that blacks are capable of treating blacks every bit as badly as whites have treated them. One friend experienced this directly in the "independent" Transkei, not only serving five and a half years in prison for organizing a political study group, but being sadistically confined to death row for part of that time. Afterwards his step-brother was murdered by the Transkei police and, when he and another step-brother protested, they were detained for thirty days. Corrupt and violent, this kind of native "self-rule" has little chance of outliving the rule of its white masters.

Tensions within the Liberation Movement

The foreign anti-apartheid movement had better prepare itself for a further shock. Like that earlier great international cause of our century, the Spanish republic, South Africa's liberation movement will one day unravel before our eyes. The fall of Winnie Mandela is a forewarning of what is to follow. There will be no reason to be disillusioned, or to lose hope, or to start complaining about being "betrayed." Indeed, realistically speaking, there is every reason to be thankful that one organization—the ANC—a handful of leaders, and a single document—the Freedom Charter—have remained hegemonic for so long. Considering the brilliant divide-and-conquer tactics of the state, the inevitable strains between an exile leadership and an in-country movement, the movement's different races and social forces, and the depth of the issues that might polarize them, it is truly remarkable that the Congress movement has remained so coherent and dominant for so long. But as I have indicated, it is by no means the whole of the South African opposition, and neither it nor the opposition is as unified as it appears from afar.

I was not in South Africa for very long when I first heard criticism of the ANC from activists in the Congress of South African Trade Unions (COSATU). This came as I was learning how deep and how widespread is the reach of this banned organization that is everywhere; even the COSATU activist was a Charterist who would have agreed that the ANC is "our" leadership. But they were criticized for wanting too much control over events in South Africa, and for not being as concerned as activists in the country to develop and nurture local leadership. They were accused by one of their partisans of expecting to come back the day after liberation and assume power over the masses in the country, ignoring the tens and hundreds of thousands of militants who will make the victory possible.

Second, I learned in Durban, and even more forcefully in Cape Town—the two places where I spent most of my time—that a significant proportion of black South Africans do *not* identify with the Congress movement and with its fundamental approaches to the questions of class alliances, the roles of whites and of the black petty bourgeoisie, and its interpretation of "non-racialism." [7] In Durban I spent time with a former national officer of the Azanian

African Students Movement (AZASM) exploring that organization's explicit working-class, socialist, and Third-World orientation. His intellectual roots lay not in the Congress movement and the Freedom Charter, but in Steve Biko's formulation of Black Consciousness, as well as in an older tradition of pan-Africanism. He put stress on the struggle between whites and blacks, as oppressors and oppressed. He refused to leave the divisive question—of the role of capitalism in a future black-ruled South Africa—for "later," because he insisted that the country cannot really *be* ruled by blacks as long as the racial capitalism at the heart of South African social and economic life prevails. Under the ANC/UDF, he argued, black political rule will disguise continued white power over black people in the most vital areas of their lives. Liberation, he emphasized, will be led only by the black working class, not by a coalition of social forces, if it is to be a liberation from racial capitalism. Such liberation entails a socialist transformation.

I was less comfortable with his analysis than with the Congress and Charterist orientation of most of those I met. Certainly part of my discomfort turned on the fact that the Black Consciousness, as opposed to the Charterist, tendency within the liberation movement rules out a role for people like myself. I was not the only white to remark that Communist party leader Joe Slovo's position on the executive of the ANC pays homage not only to the ANC's commitment to a non-racial future but also to the importance of whites in the struggle to achieve it. Moreover, even if it is "petty bourgeois" in character, I tend to agree with the ANC's insistence that only a coalition of races and classes will bring about majority rule. This seems to me to be based on a proper evaluation of the current balance of forces in South Africa and the world, and the nature of the anti-apartheid support movement. To put this more sharply, what we call "human rights" today—which are, after all, the rights demanded by the Congress movement—may be dismissed by those to its left as being limited "bourgeois rights"; but these are currently the only rights that command universal support throughout the world, irrespective of social class. As the American civil rights movement discovered, support outside the black community tailed off sharply the moment that community began to, as it inevitably had to, demand *more* than formal equality and constitutionally guaranteed political freedoms. The Western world has agreed that majority rule, national self-determination, and freedom from oppression on account of race are basic human rights; it has not (yet) decided the same about food, shelter, or employment, let alone industrial, social, or economic democracy. Tactically and strategically speaking, the Congress movement has built on, and achieved, the broadest common denominator: majority rule, national self-determination, opposition to racism as such.

But as I remarked above, this has not been enough to bring down apartheid. Even the seemingly noncontroversial character of the ANC's demands has been *too* controversial to win support from the countries that matter the most. Today it is almost as difficult to imagine how white South Africa would surrender power to an ANC-led coalition as it is to imagine the victory of socialism in South Africa. Moreover, as I suggested in chapter 5, capitalism and apartheid have been inextricably connected in the past and, as I will discuss below, remain so intertwined in the present that it will be difficult, if not impossible, to create a capitalist South Africa without apartheid. Thus one can speak convincingly of racial capitalism. And it is not easy to respond effectively to the telling question: What kind of majority rule will it be if the minority continues to control the economic life of black South Africans? With these considerations added together, in other words, the ANC/UDF does not have a monopoly on persuasive, sophisticated analysis of the situation in South Africa. The National Forum perspective is politically impressive, and in any case remains a powerful, if minority, current within black life.[8]

A Capitalist or a Socialist Future?

Inevitably, then, a major area of conflict in the post-apartheid state, no less than in the process of getting there, will be over its tilt towards capitalism or socialism. It is worth noting that the Congress movement has remained ambiguous on the question. Although the Freedom Charter, adopted in 1955, calls for the mines, the banks, and monopoly industry be taken over by "the people as a whole," Nelson Mandela himself saw the nationalizations as leading to the development of a non-European bourgeoisie.[9] On the other hand, a UDF pamphlet envisions the step after the nationalizations as placing "control of the commanding heights of the country's economy in the hands of the people, particularly the working people. The products and wealth will then be planned and shared so that the people as a whole benefit." [10]

While debate continues about the meaning and anticipated pace of such changes, a visitor to South Africa cannot help but be struck by the extent to which socialist and Marxist ideas form a major pole of discussion about South Africa's future. This is true both in the universities and in the townships. The National Forum and AZAPO, its major constituent organization, have played an important role in sharpening the critique of capitalism among the black masses and in spreading the sense that only with socialism will South Africa's racial capitalism be decisively ended. In the universities, the connections between apartheid and capitalism are much discussed and debated; in the townships, the common experience, as one African woman told me, is that "capitalism and apartheid are inseparable." Her people's dominant experience, even with the most recent reforms, remains one of being kept as a vast labor reserve for white-owned farms, mines, and factories, producing enormous profits for them, and receiving a fraction of white wages.

That she saw the connection as self-evident explains the current effort by major corporations to distance themselves from apartheid, and equally suggests how enormous are the obstacles this effort faces. Even without the significant ideological formations that are already spreading socialist ideas, few blacks are likely to accept an invitation to imagine some non-existent non-racial system of free enterprise apart from their actual lived experience. After all, past and present, most have lived apartheid as a single system, suffering simultaneously at the hands of the Afrikaans-speaking state and English-speaking capital. The intimacy remains today: capital, for all its reformist urgency, has not declared for one person one vote in a unitary South Africa;[11] it opposes sanctions as does the state; it helps the state meet its security needs. For all its commitment to a non-racial South Africa as a matter of economic rationality, proclaimed in full-page advertisements in the *Weekly Mail*, for all of its charitable and educational work to better the position of blacks, for all of its multi-million dollar concern for better housing and access to employment, it can do nothing to convince blacks that it accepts majority rule, short of declaring for majority rule. In fact, as I said earlier, it is betting on both sides, and everyone knows it.

A striking example is the annual statement for 1988 by G. W. H. Relly, chairman of Anglo-American, which controls one-quarter of the South African economy. He finds that, in spite of the shortsightedness and arrogance of those calling for sanctions, "South African social-political dynamics are already working powerfully for black people." Anglo-American is unashamedly on both sides: "Everyone abhors emergency powers which so severely circumscribe the rule of law, but one is entitled to abhor just as much the mindless mayhem and murder which was prevailing in South Africa." Relly applauds President Botha *and* foresees abolition of group areas—both out of a commitment to free enterprise without excessive government interference.[12] Gradual amelioration *within* the current order: this is the message of South Africa's leading capitalist.

In addition to the presence of significant, explicit socialist currents among blacks and capital's participation in apartheid, past and present, two other reasons ensure that socialism will be placed on the agenda in a liberated South Africa. First, obvious to all, South Africa is an impressively industrialized society. Indeed, the great period of industrialization was the classical period of apartheid, suggesting a horrible "cunning of reason" behind turning the country into one vast forced-labor camp. In spite of apartheid's differential wages, and therefore the lack of any significant development of black consumption, it ranks thirtieth in the world in per capita income. The industrial giant of Africa, the country converted the profits of its gold and diamond mines into a formidable industrial apparatus after 1948. Its whites live on a par with those in the wealthiest countries in the world, and have cheap servants to boot. The longer and more bitter the process of liberation, the stronger will be the pressure to use these resources for general well-being and to honor those sections of the Freedom Charter calling for collective ownership, or to push further, towards the socialist demands of the Manifesto of the Azanian People.

Second, blacks form the overwhelming majority of the South African working class. As servants, as workers, they see the extent of what they have created, and they see how little of it they have. Millions more waste away in the homelands, without work, barely surviving. After liberation, the sheer pressure of their needs will make itself felt. No post-apartheid state will be able to ignore the pent-up hunger of the masses. They will demand everything, and at once. Moreover, the working class and its trade union federation, COSATU, will have played a major role in the fall of apartheid. Every year that passes only strengthens its place in the South African economy and in black political life, its discipline and sense of self-confidence. After the inevitable defeat of the insurrectionary wave of the middle 1980s, it is hard to imagine a renewed struggle which does not have the labor movement at or near its center.

Yet the ANC, in its pre-negotiations, has been trying to distance itself from a commitment to socialism. It has been sounding more and more reassuring to the owners of capital. Its road to power, blocked by sheer Afrikaner might, increasingly is perceived as lying through Western capitals and Johannesburg board rooms. Directly or indirectly, Mr. Relly is already negotiating with them. His price for embracing majority rule will not be modest.

Whatever the direction to liberation, already strong class and ideological differences are bound to threaten the unity of the democratic movement. As I have indicated, those advocating a different path than the ANC's moderate one are already and increasingly regarded with hostility by those close to the ANC/UDF. Although I was prepared for this tension, I was surprised by its intensity. At the University of the Western Cape, the UDF-controlled student government had managed to get AZASM banned as a student organization. Violence between the two tendencies there and elsewhere was not uncommon. I also heard many critiques of the UDF by independents: for lacking realism in urging young people into battle with the state, for authoritarianism, for organizing in a highly bureaucratic style.

No wonder then that an outsider's image of the comradeliness of anti-apartheid organizations slowly dissolved during my travels around the country, and most especially in the Western Cape. In South Africa, as with the American new left in the 1960s, "the movement" is not quite the tight-knit family one might like it to be. From afar it is invested with moral authority and a sense of total popular support; close up, it not only has its inevitable differences, but can be seen to produce its ritualized, wooden lan-

guage, its authoritarian habits, and its paranoia, as well as its tendency to magnify divisions among comrades. One young man at
the University of the Western Cape mocked these realities, and
himself, by describing himself as belonging neither to the UDF nor
AZAPO, but rather to the "extreme middle."

If current conflicts are any indication, post-apartheid South Africa is not likely to be the democracy of one's hopes. The wish
might be more realizable if the conflict between different conceptions of post-apartheid society could be carried on openly and
democratically. But the struggle is being carried out among an exile leadership under constant threat, on the one hand, and in the
country under police-state conditions, on the other. Under such
conditions, and in a society which has systematically underdeveloped its people, hoping for an open and democratic deliberation
is clearly utopian. Even so, there are those who continue to demand that issues be discussed fully, that collective decisions be
taken rather than imposed, that alternative opinions be heard
rather than silenced. However against the mainstream they are
swimming, this is one of the tasks being attempted by philosophers and other academics. In this sense philosophy has its task
cut out for it in South Africa: reason is inevitably aligned with the
movement, and inevitably critical of it.[13]

As I have suggested, the struggle over the future is also a
struggle over different ways of ending apartheid. Those who advocate a more rapid transition to socialism through more active
involvement of the working masses are no doubt seen as jeopar-
dizing support in Western capitals and among South African busi-
nessmen; those who seek to negotiate a compromise are no doubt
seen as betraying the working masses who have been bearing the
brunt of the struggle and of state repression. If internal union
struggles and verbal and physical attacks by the various tendencies
on each other are any indication, it will be a bitter and violent
struggle.

After liberation, then, we should not be surprised at authoritarian rule. A 1987 issue of the UDF journal, *Isizwe,* argues that "the
essence of democracy does not lie in [a] debating society view of
politics, but in the ability of the working masses to effectively control their lives." And this in turn rests on "united, disciplined mass
action." "Democratic involvement of all members" clearly does
not mean free and open discussion, but techniques geared to the

state of emergency: elected leadership, collective leadership, mandating, reporting back, and criticism and self-criticism. At no step are individual opinions and debates encouraged; these are presumably holdovers from the "abstract, liberal view of democracy." [14] When pressed on its plans in a variety of areas, the ANC leadership responds, "The people will decide." How? Which people, defined how? Through what channels, after what discussions?

Will It Be Worth It?

The future, it is reasonable to expect, augurs increasingly feverish efforts to reform the system while keeping effective power in white hands, an increasingly violent conflict to end apartheid, tribal struggles, class struggles and political struggles over basic democratic rights, and struggles within the movement. One of the most depressing discussions I had in South Africa concerned precisely these questions about what lies ahead. It followed dinner in a Cape Town row house reminiscent of London. Our host had been traveling around the country studying the prospects for liberal democracy by exploring the vision of the future held by each major political tendency. Because bases for negotiation were hard to find, he was discouraged about the chances for a resolution that would be qualitatively better than the present.

We explored the prospects after apartheid for several hours, sketching the future with increasing gloom: a one-party state keeping the economic ruling powers as they are, controlling the political extremes with violence, and governing its constituents by patronage. This, after all, corresponded pretty closely to how the company, black and white, would describe South Africa today. Was this great struggle, with so much suffering still ahead, fated to produce essentially the same situation? Would black socialists and trade unionists be detained under a one-party ANC/UDF state? Would an ANC/UDF government suppress free speech and distribute thousands of patronage jobs only to its loyal allies? The obvious question, left unstated, silenced everyone: If so, what was the point of it all?

"It will still be worth it," one of the guests broke the silence. "Even if everything else remains the same, one absolutely decisive evil will be removed. The humiliation of apartheid will be replaced by a non-racial society. Even if nothing else changes, it will have been worth it."

The party fell silent pondering the hope within the intolerable ambiguity. It was a slender hope indeed, barely consoling for so much pain, and yet, no one could deny it, it would also be a major human victory.

But Are They Ready?

Beneath these concerns lurks another issue, one that surfaced while our hostess in Bophuthatswana was showing us around villages with traditional Tswana thatched roofs, a sculpture workshop, the new government buildings, and the gate of the police compound. The night before, on BOP-TV, the white director of police public relations had shocked us all by a patronizing little lecture on how to avoid car theft, delivered slowly and repetitively as if by a parent to children, and we now talked about whites in high positions in the Bop government, including the defense minister (a South African) and the finance minister (a former Rhodesian). My hostess agreed that this indicated South African domination of Bophuthatswana, but then she added, referring to the finance minister: "Tswanas just aren't good at math, so it's no surprise they appointed a white."

I protested, but she insisted. I debated with myself about whether to continue to confront what I heard as racism. Unusual among whites in South Africa, this woman teaches in a black school; in fact she resigned from, and withdrew her daughters from, the Mafikeng school when it insisted on staying within the South African system (and remaining white) after a grace period expired. She and her husband were among the few thousand whites who had moved here in order to live and work among blacks, "using apartheid to undermine apartheid." I decided that her remark must be an old reflex, the expression of a habit that, whether in South Africa or the United States, the most committed person couldn't break all at once. There was no point in continuing to challenge it.

I wish I had, for my sake. What if she had insisted, from her own experience, that Tswanas generally have little success in math but perhaps excel in other areas? And what if she had accepted that this failing was due to exogenous social and historical factors, not at all to hereditary racial ones? Isn't it just possible that President Mangope might have had great difficulty recruiting someone sufficiently qualified to be finance minister from his few thousand loyalists among the less than two million Tswanas actually living in the territory? Isn't it just possible that this remark was an accurate reflection on the current educational, social, and political reality among Tswanas?

Her husband travels to rural schools in Bophuthatswana to develop programs for upgrading the skills of teachers, and describes the facilities as being among the crudest in the world, sometimes lacking proper classrooms, writing instruments, and even water. These are the kinds of issues that occupy their lives, lives absorbed in overcoming the vicious circle of Tswana "underdevelopment." Such questions consume many blacks and whites in South Africa, and suggest that for many today black development is as important as the political struggle.

Black "underdevelopment" and its relationship to racial domination, after all, is the key ambiguity I brought back with me. Its relevance is indicated by the colleague who whisked me off to the Durban market, by the wealthy lady who spoke of Brazil. "South Africa is a First-World country and a Third-World country" is their common theme, and I heard it from other whites, often in justification of apartheid. One can read it in the *Wall Street Journal* in plausible appeals by South African business for an end to sanctions. The implication is: the oppressions you see are less oppressions than the inevitable by-products of the encounter between two different cultures, one of which is, must be, must continue to be, tutor to the other. Until the blacks "catch up" and are "ready." Wasn't this the meaning of the Paul Simon interview?

The same attitude appeared unexpectedly in one of the most stimulating teaching sessions I had, on the great exposition of progress, Condorcet's *Sketch for a Historical Picture of the Progress of the Human Mind*. Writing nearly two hundred years ago, Condorcet talks about Africa at the beginning of his stirring last chapter, where he subjects the whole world, including "the barbarism of African tribes," to a prophecy of steady scientific, technological, economic, educational, and political advance. If he does not even consider non-Western values and practices (such as living in harmony with nature) as having any claim to survival, Condor-cet with equal force rejects "our treachery, our murderous con-tempt for men of another color or creed, the insolence of our usur-pations, the intrigues or the exaggerated proselytic zeal of our priests." How does the great philosopher of progress regard Asia and Africa?

These vast lands are inhabited partly by large tribes who need only assist-ance from us to become civilized, who wait only to find brothers amongst the European nations to become their friends and pupils; partly by races oppressed by sacred despots or dull-witted conquerors, and who for so many centuries have cried out to be liberated; partly by tribes living in a condition of almost total savagery in a climate whose harshness repels the sweet bless-ings of civilization and deters those who would teach them its benefits; and finally, by conquering hordes who know no other law but force, no other profession but piracy. The progress of these two last classes of people will be slower and stormier; and perhaps it will even be that, reduced in number as they are driven back by civilized nations, they will finally disappear imper-ceptibly before them or merge into them.[15]

As one student pointed out, Condorcet cannot even concep-tualize Asia and Africa without seeing them through the conde-scending lenses of progress. Their differences become deficiencies. These lenses impose not only their own terms of judgment but, ultimately, a death sentence on non-European cultures. From tu-telage to genocide, the project has indeed been carried out. It rules the world. It was enforced, and thus "made true," by European physical power. Its being carried out meant cultural transforma-tion and domination by Western habits, values, and institutions. All the students I spoke with agreed that today, more than ever, the agenda for the whole world is set by Western technical and economic "progress." To survive has come to mean to "catch up" in education, science, technology, contemporary work skills. Black students want to use these skills for liberation, attacking the West on its own ground, with its own values, using its own techniques.

Still, all of us, except possibly for the students at the University of the Western Cape who challenged the whole notion of progress, are trapped in a logic that legitimizes the vicious question: "Are they ready?" After all, it seems patently obvious that survival in today's world requires a certain level of education, skills, training, habits—a certain level of "development." There are only two problems: achieving it is as much an imprisonment as a liberation, and the deck is so stacked that virtually no people under Western domination can achieve it.

First, the tone of judgment we see in Condorcet combines the unhesitating belief that it is *better* to be more "developed" with confidence in being able to impose this on others. It is remarkable, in the twentieth century, that anyone can still be as arrogant as Condorcet was in the eighteenth about a Western progress that has destroyed cultures, deteriorated the environment, perfected genocide, and threatens the planet. Condorcet's optimistic hopes foreshadowed enormous technical and social progress in the West but also unmitigated catastrophes and the prospect of more. Every gain can be balanced by a loss. It may well be that the West can still pass through the eye of the needle and convert its disastrous progress into liberation. So far, however, it remains highly debatable whether "development" has improved human life as such; only a breakthrough to radically new social systems, perhaps partially guided by non-Western values, might make it all worthwhile.

One of the key reasons for Western progress, and the source of the immiseration of the rest of the world, has been the continuing, catastrophic encounter between the capitalist West and peoples of color. As Immanuel Wallerstein argues, "The overwhelming proportion of the world's work-forces, who live in rural zones or move between them and urban slums, are worse off than their ancestors five hundred years ago."[16] They are still caught in the yoke we fitted them with, the long nightmare of oppression from which none of us has yet awakened.

The talk of lack of "development," genuine enough in comparative economic and technical terms, really points to *arrested* development under Western domination.[17] "Are they ready?" is a mischievous, hypocritical question, worthy of those who cripple others and then decide they are unfit to walk. Morally, everyone is ready to live free; politically, they will do so as they wrest control from those whose power permits them to ask the question. Typical of colonialism everywhere, white South Africa has provided little training to make blacks "ready"; many of those today who assert the right have gotten themselves ready by educating themselves in struggle, in exile, or in what many regard, both ironically and romantically, but perhaps also with a grain of truth, as the country's greatest university, Robben Island.

But are they ready? I actually foreshadowed my answer shortly before leaving for South Africa. One day, lost in thoughts on "progress," "development," and "underdevelopment," I entered a Detroit church for a meeting on South Africa and was jolted by a speech by Reverend Maurice Ngakane, a South African exile. Reverend Ngakane confronted me with the opposite of any conceivable black "developmental inferiority" to whites, a kind of moral strength I have seen mostly in people of color (for historical, not racial reasons). He spoke with the dignity and generosity of the oppressed, making words like "freedom" and "love" sound real once more. His talk showed an integration of mind and heart. He spoke of his own people's freedom, but his vision tied their liberation to the liberation of all of humankind. Ringing out in that black church six blocks from where I was born in the center of a city half-destroyed by racism, his words returned me, embarrassed, to my questions. Underdevelopment? Technical inferiority? I was abruptly jostled from what suddenly felt like immersion in racist stereotypes, and returned to a sense of deep respect for the moral and political qualities developed by the people suffering from white domination. After all, this century's great moral leaders—for all of us—have been the Gandhis, the Kings, the Mandelas.

In South Africa, I experienced this same large spirit time and again. Regardless of race, and in spite of apartheid, the South Africans I met were uncommonly gracious: some sense of common humanity has survived the brutalization. Whatever its problems and weaknesses may be, the movement reflects this generous temper. Not only has the liberation struggle not become a race war, but the commitment to ultimate reconciliation between blacks and whites was present in every opponent of apartheid I spoke with. Whether they referred to the consciously non-racial character of the Freedom Charter and the governing slogan of "One person, one vote in a unitary South Africa," or to the Manifesto of the Azanian People and Steve Biko's "Black man, you're on your own," South African blacks are—remarkably—clear that the fundamental problem is not South African whites. This anti-racist commitment seems to be value and operating principle, for example in the daily functioning of anti-apartheid organizations and in peer relationships between white and black activists (including relationships of mutual respect between blacks committed to

Black Consciousness and whites). However various tendencies may interpret it, the agreed-upon goal of the liberation movement is a non-racial South Africa. No one I spoke to doubted that whites too are Africans, and have a place in the future free South Africa. At this moment in history the enemy is not whites, but apartheid.

All of this points to a conclusion as simple as it is difficult to achieve. The situation in South Africa demands majority rule. The fact that black South Africans rise up to demand freedom is the best argument that they are ready for freedom. The fact that black South Africans demand power is the best argument that they are ready for power. They have signaled that readiness with a remarkable generosity.

And if their generosity does not prevail? If the struggle becomes so brutal as to lead to large-scale civil war, massive white flight, and the destruction of South Africa's economy? If South Africa is liberated only after a fight to the finish, the country may well face disaster. The crystal clarity of the need to end racial oppression may well give way to a society in ruins, as the ambiguities I have been speaking about may yield to real historical catastrophes.

Will this be the choice—a liberated society in ruins or rule by a racial minority? Will this be the final bitter fruit of white rule? Three hundred years of white domination have been a continuing catastrophe, most recently in the form of the oppression, humiliation, and intentionally arrested development known as apartheid. Whatever happens from here on in this beautiful, rich part of the world, let it finally be in the name of the majority.

Postscript: Power, Violence; Music, Love

If apartheid is about anything relatively simple, it is about power. Above I spoke of the power of a small group of once-vanquished people to redefine human reality according to their own social, political, and economic needs. Equally obvious in South Africa is the power of those who dominate economically to level all merely human barriers to pursuing their interest in maximizing profit and controlling labor. One Saturday in Durban we were taken on a tour of South Africa's power: its train stations, its port, its factories and refineries, and afterward its splendid neighborhoods where those who enjoy these kinds of power have their homes, followed by the police compound where the power is protected and those challenging it are questioned and detained.

The sense of power was most palpable at the city's new railroad station, one of the world's largest. Fortress-like, its unrelieved massiveness suggests how important rail travel is to apartheid: enough to command vast spaces and enormous resources, and to require great architectural monuments. Together with the commuter station near the Indian market, this place funnels much of Durban's labor from the townships of KwaZulu to the factories, port, hotels, offices, shops, and homes of Durban. An overbearing and cheerless statement in concrete and glass, it also testifies to the power of the state to redefine reality. All traces of overt racism have been expunged: not so much as a sign directing blacks here, or reserving this space for whites. Nevertheless, it is divided, quite starkly, into two totally separate passenger levels, one for commuters and second-class passengers, the other for long-distance and first-class passengers. A separation is effected rationally, in terms of traffic flow, without offending the sensitive eye. On a Saturday afternoon as we explored its ridiculously monumental halls, a few whites were in the long-distance room and, a world away, a crowd of blacks sat on their baggage in the local room.

"Do not underestimate our fist of iron." [1]

If the new Durban rail station shows one side of white power in today's South Africa, this statement is a threat to use violent, repressive power, the kind suggested by the police compound. They are the words of the minister of law and order, Adriaan Vlok, in response to an article in the *Times* of London. That article was about Chris Hani, chief-of-staff of Umkhonto we Sizwe, the military wing of the African National Congress. It might equally be a response to my suggestion in chapter 5 that an essential impotence underlies apartheid.

Chris Hani has himself felt the power that the minister is threatening. Only by climbing out of a back window while South African military units were breaking down the front door did he manage to survive their devastating raid into Maseru, Lesotho, in December 1982. Had he not escaped, he would have been one of the over forty people, thirty of them members of the ANC, who were killed.

This violent, repressive power of the state was one of my two dominant impressions of South Africa. Above I mentioned some examples—knowing in advance that conditions were attached to my being able to visit, speaking and living under the threat of surveillance, talking with people who had been imprisoned or detained, meeting with people in hiding, talking about friends and relatives who had been murdered. My memorial lecture to Richard Turner was ended, with terrible appropriateness, by an announcement that the chair of SANSCO, the black student group I had met with three weeks earlier, had been detained. A police helicopter "observed" a rally at a campus I was lecturing at; the rally itself protested an execution. My last two weeks at South African universities were clouded by the general shock about, and response to, new regulations designed to control such student political activity.

After my return home the picture only worsened. Immediately after the new university regulations were set aside by the courts, the state severely slashed university budgets. The fist of iron struck down ANC representative Dulcie September in Paris, and blew off Albie Sachs's hand in Maputo. Mozambique continued to stagger from the bestial attacks by a terrorist movement generally agreed to have been started, guided, and financed by the South African state. The editor of the newspaper the *New Nation* was kept in detention nearly two years; the paper was forced to suspend publication for three months; the *Weekly Mail* was also suspended. All of the major anti-apartheid political organizations were "restricted"—a newspeak category just short of being outlawed, which prohibits them from engaging in any activity. More individuals were "banned"—removed from politics by being prohibited from speaking, writing, or attending any public or private meetings.

"Do not underestimate our fist of iron."

My wife and I had visited Portland Place in Johannesburg, hoping to find a minister I had met in Detroit. He was away at a conference, but at this bustling religious center, home to church-related anti-apartheid activity, we did manage to speak to a young Indian man. We were able to find a small space where we could talk for a little while. Its political posters, informality, and obvious energy made this place appealing. The young man left us with inspiring words: "People are starting to believe that they are human beings. When they do they'll accept no less than being treated as human beings. They won't stop until they achieve that. No matter how long it takes." Perhaps it was the depth of his conviction, perhaps his natural friendliness; but we made a strong connection, and our brief exchange was one of the memorable moments of our trip.

A year later, on August 31, 1988, we read that a church center in Johannesburg was destroyed in an explosion shortly after 1 A.M., and twenty-three people were wounded. A bomb, expertly placed in the garage beneath the building, blew off the facade, made a hole in the roof, and collapsed the lobby into the basement. Anti-apartheid leaders blamed government agents for the attack. If the state did not commission it, it was certainly the work of trained vigilantes with access to sophisticated explosives. In any case, it was only the latest in a series of such attacks against anti-apartheid organizations, church groups, and labor unions.

My first thought was that this building, Khotso House, was the place we had visited; it was not. Yet the shock, outrage, and pain we felt from a distance of six thousand miles was not really eased when we realized that our young friend and his colleagues were safe. They might be next; others, equally devoted and courageous, were on the receiving end this time. Everyone we knew in South Africa was hurt by the bomb, and we hurt for them.

"Do not underestimate our fist of iron."

My second dominant impression of South Africa was of the spirit of these people who are struggling against the fist of iron: "They won't stop. . . . No matter how long it takes." The young man's words have been translated into an entire culture, white and black, of such depth and breadth, of such strong morale, that it will not be destroyed by any amount of bannings or restrictions or detentions or bombings or killings. White or black, one could easily spend one's entire life in this culture. I asked one white academic to introduce me to defenders of apartheid; after some hesitation, he confessed that he really didn't know any. His world, after all, is an anti-apartheid one. The vast majority of the people of South Africa live in its various and overlapping anti-apartheid worlds.

Certainly the repression is stifling, demobilizing, demoralizing. But even under conditions of intense repression, the majority see a number of things from which to take heart. First, they continue to force concessions from the state, in spite of its ruthlessness. Even if they avoid the key issue, of power, the concessions only make the majority more determined. Second, in small ways and in big, often hypocritically but often materially, the world is on their side. Third, there are real limits to repression: although it was banned twenty-five years ago, the African National Congress is present everywhere in South Africa. Illegal, it commands the loyalty of the majority of South Africans.

Above all, they *are* the majority, and they know it. They know, and every rational person in South Africa knows, that majority rule is inevitable. Whatever power the state exercises today or tomorrow, however it may increase that power, in the long run it can only delay the inevitable. Where does the self-pity and bluster of the defenders of apartheid come from, if not from a sense of ultimate doom? A deep conviction pervades the majority in South Africa, on the other hand, because they know they are right. No matter how long it takes, they know they will be free.

This is the outer limit of the state's power. In the end, the moral force of the majority, translated into morale, matters more. The racial state can invent no strategy to win the majority's support, neutralize its leaders, or win its passive acquiescence. And without these, ultimately, no modern state has a future. Its staying power springs not from physical power but from legitimacy. Sharpeville, the Soweto uprising of 1976, and the mass movement of 1984–86 were the majority's response to ever more feverish white efforts to restore a collapsing legitimacy. Clearly, the racial state and racial capitalism can no longer remain racial and be accepted as legitimate by South Africa's majority. In such a situation, every effort at cooptation—every new work skill attained, every middle-class home built in a township, every managerial position achieved, every mind that becomes exposed to higher education—becomes another living contradiction, another source of black rage, another potential black leader or sympathizer. In the end, force cannot replace loyalty, and loyalty to such a social order is impossible.

"They won't stop. . . . No matter how long it takes."

I felt this most strongly in experiences of listening to music. During my last hours before leaving Durban, several friends took me to the Rainbow Restaurant in Pinetown to hear Philip Tabane and Malombo. Tabane uses contemporary electric guitars, but the other members of his group play traditional African percussion instruments, including large cowhide drums that have to be heated during breaks to regain their suppleness and tone.

In this packed club on a Sunday afternoon the obvious freedom and sense of celebration between the musicians and the audience, and equally within the audience, did not divert from the power of the music, but rather allowed the music to claim all of its meanings, from the most technical to the most fully human. It was inventive, sophisticated black music, self-consciously seeking to ground itself in African experience. What did it mean that an interracial audience was listening to a black guitarist searching for African roots, and taking the search as its own? What did it mean that on the deepest level the music was at the same time an expression of black suffering and joy and yet a universal song? While being fully itself, the music spoke about, and we seemed to live intensely, another world.

As we listened to it in a setting where everyone in the room shared it with everyone else, I think we had a sense not just of a moment's relief from conflict, not just of lifting ourselves beyond apartheid, but, briefly, of liberation.[2] Amidst the threatening social madness, we experienced social happiness. Sharing this experience, with friends I had connected with powerfully, I acutely felt the sense of solidarity and love that had so marked my time in South Africa.

One man, also a philosopher, and I looked at each other knowingly. We had argued over Plato earlier in my stay.

"This is the good," I whispered. We laughed.

Two weeks before, I had an equally joyous encounter with this spirit, which has since merged with my most painful experience of South Africa. It began with a moment of anxiety in the winter darkness of downtown Johannesburg, which was over before I could even say what it was I had begun to fear. The car pulled into the empty parking lot where the airport bus had left me, David Webster and Maggie Friedman greeted me as if we were old friends, and we drove off to David's office at the University of the Witwatersrand to use the phone. We would spend Saturday evening and Sunday morning together, for the sole reason that a mutual friend in Durban had said we "must" meet each other. While David was making reservations at a favorite Portuguese restaurant, I looked over his bookshelves and noticed how parallel, and how equally political, were our interests, in spite of his academic home in social anthropology and mine in philosophy.

At a dinner served, ironically, by refugees from majority rule in Portuguese Africa, we got to know each other by discussing the prospects for majority rule in South Africa—and how David and Maggie were aiding that process as whites who interact in a daily way with blacks in the democratic movement, living out, directly and personally, their commitment to a nonracial society.

We talked easily and explored the current situation. David spoke about the process in which, each time the state bans an organization, another one springs up. Now, for example, they were active in the Five Freedoms Forum (named for Roosevelt's Four Freedoms—from want, fear, of speech and association, of conscience, as well as the freedom from discrimination). Maggie spoke about how skilled whites were needed in the struggle against apartheid; for example, her own work with computers had been important for the Detainees' Parents Support Committee (it has since been restricted). As was the case whenever I was with politically active South Africans, our time together was one long, intense conversation, punctuated by normal-life activities such as eating or sleeping. In this process David Webster's special qualities emerged. No doubt he was a leader, and no doubt he had keen analytical powers. But I saw something else: a sense of calm that was not diminished by his determination, an ability to be relaxed and unafraid that was not overpowered by his total commitment to ending apartheid, a quality of humility and soft-spokenness that was not overcome by the importance of what he was doing.

After dinner, David and Maggie took me to Kippee's. A jazz club located in the Market, it featured saxophonist Basil Coetzee and his group, Sebenza. As at the Rainbow two weeks later, it was an experience of black musicians and an integrated audience, many of them being political activists. As at the Rainbow, the music was wonderful; it was African, and universal. David and Maggie introduced me to a few activist friends, but mostly we enjoyed the place, the people, and the jazz. Somewhere absorbed in the music, under the authority of its black creators, David and Maggie, myself, the whole audience, were all sharing the future, a free South Africa.

Back home in an unpretentious lower-middle-class house (whose servants' quarters in the yard went unused), David played "Graceland" and we talked some more, this time about state repression. And then I went to sleep, thumbing through the Harare *Herald*s stacked alongside my bed. David woke me early to go jogging, and we ran across the top of an abandoned gold mine. After our workout he stopped at a store to drop off some posters announcing a meeting of the Five Freedoms Forum.

Several times in the months since visiting David and Maggie I have thought about them, about their quiet calm, their humaneness. I have been struck by how normal their life was, within and alongside of their commitment: dinner at a good restaurant, followed by jazz, David and I and his dogs going jogging (Maggie played field hockey that morning); David putting up posters announcing a political meeting, followed by their trip to spend the afternoon with family (some of whom were visiting from Zimbabwe). Why did this normality captivate me so? It was the normality of an exemplary life in a grotesquely abnormal world, a normality asserted against South Africa by people determined to transform it.

It turns out that David Webster had much to be afraid of. On

Monday, May Day, 1989, he had just come back with his dogs, probably from jogging across that same abandoned gold mine. In front of his house, with Maggie watching, David was gunned down by unknown assailants. He died immediately.

"It is a rare event indeed when such assassinations are solved,"[3] David had written in a report finished just before his death. In the report he named eight activists killed by "unknown perpetrators" between September 1987 and July 1988. No one yet knows whether these murders, and David's, are the direct results of state policy, the "fist of iron," or of a growing, irrational, violence on the Right. In either case, the scenario remains the same. The police are unable to track down the murderers; the anti-apartheid movement in South Africa suspects police complicity. David's colleagues, white and black, continue to plead with the rest of the world, yet one more time, to understand that such brutality is the real face of all the proclaimed reforms of apartheid.

Notes

Preface

1. Apartheid may go, "but in an orderly way, not through a Marxist revolution or as the result of foreign pressure," concluded an officer in the South African Defense Forces in the *New York Times* (Wednesday, August 24, 1988, 4).

2. According to the Indicator Project of the University of Natal, 4,012 South Africans died in political violence between September 1984 and December 1988. At least 1,113 of these were township residents killed by the police and military (*New York Times,* Sunday, March 5, 1989, 4).

3. This report is quoted in the *Sunday Times* (Johannesburg), May 7, 1989, 7.

Introduction

1. O'Brien had been invited by the University of Cape Town in June 1987. He not only violated the British boycott, but publicly denounced it, infuriating black students at the university. They disrupted his appearances, and the resulting conflict between the state, the university, and the anti-apartheid movement created considerable tension about the issue of foreign lecturers in South Africa.

2. W. R. Sherwood, "Morality Is Crux," Letter to the Editor of the *New York Times,* August 24, 1988, 24.

3. For my discussion of this dimension of Sartre's thought, see my *Jean-Paul Sartre—Philosophy in the World* (London, 1980), 157–213.

4. Some African students are housed in the township of Umlazi, which is part of KwaZulu and under the control of Gatsha Buthelezi and his Inkatha movement.

5. South African terminology is puzzling at best. While to Americans, "multiracial" has positive anti-racist connotations, in the current language of apartheid it suggests the kind of pluralist, segregated society of official ideologists. "Nonracial" is widely accepted among those opposed to apartheid as being free of the stigma of imposed racial identities.

6. In 1985, average tertiary enrollment reached the following rates for South Africa's racial groups:
Whites: 31.3 of every 1,000
Indians: 21.3 of every 1,000
"Coloreds": 4.6 of every 1,000
Africans: 2.6 of every 1,000
This means that the total black college and university enrollment is consider-

ably less than that of whites, who constitute well under 20 percent of the population. However, white enrollment is shrinking and black enrollment is growing by leaps and bounds, a fact which points to black majorities at the English-language universities in the foreseeable future. See the *Chronicle of Higher Education,* January 11, 1989, A39.

7. The Publications Control Board can ban materials in two different ways. The less harsh one is to prohibit distribution, but not possession; if an item is banned according to the Internal Security Act, even possession is prohibited.

Chapter One

1. The network, however, has been breaking down recently. For an account of its limits and its recent deterioration, especially in the townships, see Stephen Davis, *Apartheid's Rebels* (New Haven, 1987).

2. This project will be explored below in chapter 5.

3. While I was there, a student at Cape Town confessed to his NUSAS colleagues that he was a government agent. The state had recruited him while still in secondary school, paid his fees, and had given him a monthly stipend to infiltrate student political activity. One newspaper photograph showed him at the head of a demonstration, rock in hand.

4. See Joha Louw-Potgieter, *Afrikaner Dissidents: A Social Psychological Study of Identity and Dissent* (Clevedon, England, 1988).

Chapter Two

1. KwaZulu is regarded as a "self-governing national state" which has not yet been granted independence. In this respect it resembles QwaQwa in the eastern Orange Free State; KwaNgwane, KwaNdebele, and Lebowa in the Transvaal; as well as Gazankulu. On the other hand, the Ciskei, the Transkei, Venda, and Bophuthatswana are all officially described as "independent national states." Taken together, these "homelands," or bantustans, comprise the 13 percent of South Africa set aside in 1910 as the "tribal reserves" where Africans were to be allowed to live permanently. Only recently have blacks begun to be allowed to purchase their homesites in the townships officially belonging to South Africa. See Barbara Rogers, *Divide and Rule: South Africa's Bantustans* (London, 1980).

2. See Aziza Seedat, *Crippling a Nation: Health in Apartheid South Africa* (London, 1984), 63–96.

3. "Prog" is the Progressive Federal party, an anti-apartheid party traditionally supported by English-speaking liberals. In 1987 it was displaced as the official opposition by the Conservative party. It has since merged with other liberal currents to form the Democratic party.

Chapter Three

1. See George M. Kren and Leon Rappoport, *The Holocaust and the Crisis of Human Behavior* (New York, 1980), 133–43.

2. See Stanley Milgram, *Obedience to Authority* (New York, 1974) and Kren

and Rappoport, *The Holocaust,* 68–72. The claim of obeying orders was the main defense given before the Nuremburg War Crimes Tribunal, and was Adolph Eichmann's main defense as well. See Hannah Arendt, *Eichmann in Jerusalem* (New York, 1965), 135–50.

3. Richard Wasserstrom, "The Relevance of Nuremburg," *War and Moral Responsibility* (Princeton, 1974).

4. Charter of the International Military Tribunal, August 8, 1945, in Jay W. Baird, ed., *From Nuremburg to My Lai* (Lexington, Mass., 1972), 13.

5. See Sanford Levinson, "Responsibility for Crimes of War," *War and Moral Responsibility.*

6. Jaspers is quoted in Richard A. Falk, Gabriel Kolko, and Robert Jay Lifton, eds., *Crimes of War* (New York, 1971), 477.

7. Ibid.

8. See Aristotle, *Nichomachean Ethics,* III, 1–5, in *The Basic Works of Aristotle,* ed. Richard McKeon (New York, 1941), 964–74.

9. Jean-Paul Sartre, *The Emotions: Outline of a Theory* (New York, 1948), 12.

10. Jean-Paul Sartre, *Being and Nothingness* (New York, 1956), 556.

11. Even so, it might be asked, what if we are ordered to participate in an evil process under threat of punishment for refusing? Is this a case where "moral choice" is impossible? This question is explored by Wasserstrom, "The Relevance of Nuremburg," 144–46.

12. Ibid., 138–39.

13. Ibid., 148–49.

14. Our guide to Sartre will be Thomas Flynn, *Sartre and Marxist Existentialism* (Chicago, 1983).

15. Jean-Paul Sartre, *Anti-Semite and Jew* (New York, 1948), 135–36; cited in Flynn, 55.

16. Jean-Paul Sartre, *Situations,* V (Paris, 1964), 58; Flynn, 60; quotation completed and translation changed.

17. Jean-Paul Sartre, Preface to Franz Fanon, *The Wretched of the Earth* (New York, 1968), 13; Flynn, 63.

18. Ibid., 25; Flynn, 63.

19. Sartre, *Situations,* V, 66; Flynn, 61; quotation completed.

20. Jean-Paul Sartre, *Critique of Dialectical Reason,* I (London, 1976), 761; Flynn, 160.

21. "Nazi" is substituted for *bourgeois.*

22. Raul Hilberg, *The Destruction of the European Jews* (New York, 1979), 703–15.

23. Rudolf Höss, commandant of Auschwitz, estimated that the ratio there of administrators to guards was 1:6. See Hilberg, *Destruction,* 575 n.5.

24. "His or her": women, relatively powerless and depoliticized then, would certainly have to be considered *less* responsible than men.

25. Herbert Fingarette, *The Self in Transformation* (New York, 1963), 164–65.

26. Relly quoted in Merle Lipton, *Capitalism and Apartheid* (Aldershot, England, 1985), 128.

27. Ibid., 305.

28. Ibid.

29. Military arm of the African National Congress.

30. Or even applaud: see the statement of Anglo American's Relly in chapter 6 below.

31. See chapters 5 and 6 below.

Chapter Four

1. "Hints of Hope: Afrikaners Begin to Unbend," *Time,* May 4, 1987, 22–32.

2. Theodor W. Adorno, "Progress," *The Philosophical Forum* 15, nos. 1–2 (Fall-Winter, 1983–84):55.

3. Immanuel Wallerstein, *Historical Capitalism* (London, 1983), 102.

4. The quote is in Lucy Dawidowicz, *The War against the Jews* (New York, 1975), 451.

Chapter Five

1. In opposition to most Marxist analysts of the tie between apartheid and capitalism, Merle Lipton argues that this is the goal towards which the major industrial and commercial capitalists have been pressuring—against white labor and the state bureaucracy. See her *Capitalism and Apartheid.*

2. Broadly speaking, the state's very significant stake in the economy evolved (1) to control the flow of black labor in the interests of white agriculture, mining, and labor, (2) to develop Afrikaner-controlled business, and (3) to create industries vital to the defense of white-ruled South Africa.

3. Clem Sunter, *The World and South Africa in the 1990s* (Cape Town, 1987), 105.

4. Mike Morris and Vishnu Padayachee, "State Reform Policy in South Africa," *Transformation* 7 (1988): 24.

5. See, for example, Tom Lodge, *Black Politics in South Africa Since 1945* (London, 1983), 91–113, 147–51.

6. See Elaine Unterhalter, *Forced Removal: The Division, Segregation and Control of the People of South Africa* (London, 1987), 142.

7. From the *Rand Daily Mail* in 1983, quoted in Julie Frederikse, *South Africa: A Different Kind of War* (Johannesburg, 1986), 109.

8. Lipton presents a non-Marxist version of this; for a Marxist one, see John S. Saul and Stephen Gelb, *Crisis in South Africa* (New York, 1981).

9. Such dynamics are explored in various ways in such works as Leonard Thompson, *The Political Mythology of Apartheid* (New Haven, 1985), and Heribert Adam and Herman Giliomee, *Ethnic Power Mobilized* (New Haven, 1979).

10. See my *The Dialectics of Disaster: A Preface to Hope* (London, 1983).

11. See my "Social Madness," in Isidor Walliman and Michael Dobkowski, eds., *Genocide and the Modern Age* (New York, 1987).

12. See the quote from a SADF officer above, p. 157 n. 1 (Preface).

13. This is a main point of the study by Howard Simson, *The Social Origins of Afrikaner Fascism and Its Apartheid Policy* (Stockholm, 1980).

14. Indeed, this entire discussion also implies that a normative sense is inherent in social life itself; that (even in oppressive societies) in normal times, under normal circumstances, human reality can be grasped more or less correctly and is more or less respected, even by ruling classes; and that ruling groups "normally" develop projects that more or less pay heed to human limits and possibilities. This is one of the conditions for their retaining hegemony. Indeed, the explanation of a revolutionary situation, as in South Africa today, is that the ruling classes have ceased to do so, and that great masses of people subjected to their rule have begun to contest their hegemony.

15. See Giliomee, "The Afrikaner Economic Advance," in Adam and Giliomee, *Ethnic Power.*

16. All are discussed at length in Dan O'Meara, *Volkskapitalisme* (Cambridge, 1983).

17. H. J. and R. E. Simons, *Class and Color in South Africa* (Harmondsworth, 1969), 618.

18. Lipton, *Capitalism and Apartheid,* 188.

19. Ibid., 285.

Chapter Six

1. See Ian Phillips, "Negotiation and Armed Struggle in Contemporary South Africa," *Transformation* 6 (1988).

2. The only major appeal of the state is to anti-Communism, which is a bit ironic, considering that not only do the vast majority of its people *not* have the citizenship rights of any Soviet citizen but its enterprise, not "free," is among the most heavily state-controlled in the capitalist world. The American leaders who could honor Pakistan's Zia as a "great friend of freedom" thought the same of South Africa's Botha. That is to say, he was an ally in the Cold War.

3. Lyle Tatum, ed. *South Africa: Challenge and Hope* (New York, 1987), 135.

4. As I argued in chapter 3, those at the apex of chains of command which murder innocent civilians are indeed most responsible for those murders, fully deserving of being judged guilty by history. If terrorism has any meaning, those who gave the orders for contra terror in Nicaragua are themselves terrorists.

5. See Sunter, *South Africa,* 104, and the annual report for 1988 of Anglo-American chairman G. W. H. Relly. Those who advocate sanctions "choose to ignore the reality that the result of their activities to date has been to set back reform and impoverish the people they are intended to help" (*Weekly Mail,* July 29 to August 4, 1988, 16). But for the black view, which is heavily pro-sanctions, see Mark Orkin, *The Struggle and the Future: What Black South Africans Really Think* (Johannesburg, 1986).

6. Although I quote from the American Friends Service Committee's position on washing one's hands of apartheid, their appreciation of violence in South Africa is more informed and intelligent than either those who reflexively reject or accept political violence (see Tatum, *South Africa,* 157–67).

7. See Martin Murray, *South Africa: Time of Agony, Time of Destiny* (London, 1987), 229–38, for a lucid discussion of these differences.

8. The theoretical basis for Black Consciousness is developed by Sam C. Nolutshungu, *Changing South Africa* (Cape Town, 1983).

9. Lodge, *Black Politics in South Africa since 1945*, 71–73, and Nelson Mandela, *The Struggle Is My Life* (New York, 1986), 50–58.

10. *UDF Focus on the Freedom Charter* (pamphlet).

11. Sunter calls vaguely for "joint negotiations with give-and-take on all
sides" and "genuine democracy in which every single person can participate."
But even if his vision is to "negotiate a future with all who would participate in
it," he is not willing to specify that this means majority rule. The book jacket
shows what he looks like, and tells us that "his hobbies include music and
golf"—but not the decisive answer to the decisive question. And he is, after all,
talking about *The World and South Africa in the 1990s* (106–8).

12. *Weekly Mail,* July 29 to August 4, 1988, 16–17.

13. For a discussion of the role of philosophy in South Africa today, see M. A.
Nupen, "Philosophy and the Crisis in South Africa," *Transformation* 7 (1988).

14. "Democracy," *Isizwe: The Nation.*

15. Antoine-Nicolas de Condorcet, *Sketch for a Historical Picture of the Progress of the Human Mind* (Westport, Conn., 1979), 177.

16. Wallerstein, *Historical Capitalism,* 101.

17. See Walter Rodney, *How Europe Underdeveloped Africa* (Washington,
D. C., 1982).

Postscript

1. *Weekly Mail,* June 10 to June 15, 1988, 5.

2. The great tradition of modern aesthetics returns again and again to the
theme that art foreshadows an alternative reality. As Herbert Marcuse says, "Art
breaks open a dimension inaccessible to other experience, a dimension in which
human beings, nature, and things no longer stand under the law of the established reality principle. Subjects and objects encounter the appearance of that
autonomy which is denied them in their society" (*The Aesthetic Dimension* [Bos-
ton, 1978], 72).

3. This report is quoted in the *Sunday Times* (Johannesburg), May 7, 1989,
7.

Bibliography

Adam, Heribert, and Herman Giliomee. *Ethnic Power Mobilized: Can South Africa Change?* New Haven, 1979.

Adorno, Theodor W. "Progress," *The Philosophical Forum* 15, nos. 1–2 (Fall-Winter, 1983–84).

Arendt, Hannah. *Eichmann in Jerusalem.* New York, 1965.

Aristotle. *Nichomachean Ethics.* In *The Basic Works of Aristotle,* ed. Richard McKeon. New York, 1941.

Aronson, Ronald. *The Dialectics of Disaster: A Preface to Hope.* London, 1983.

———. *Jean-Paul Sartre—Philosophy in the World.* London, 1980.

———. "Social Madness." In Isidor Walliman and Michael Dobkowski, eds. *Genocide and the Modern Age.* New York, 1987.

Attwell, Michael. *South Africa.* London, 1986.

Baird, Jay W., ed. *From Nuremburg to My Lai.* Lexington, Mass., 1972.

Cole, Josette. *Crossroads: The Politics of Reform and Repression, 1976–1986.* Cape Town, 1987.

Condorcet, Antoine-Nicolas de. *Sketch for a Historical Picture of the Progress of the Human Mind.* Westport, Conn., 1979.

Davis, Stephen M. *Apartheid's Rebels.* New Haven, 1987.

Dawidowicz, Lucy. *The War against the Jews.* New York, 1975.

Diepen, Maria van, ed. *The National Question in South Africa.* London, 1988.

Falk, Richard A., Gabriel Kolko, and Robert Jay Lifton, eds. *Crimes of War.* New York, 1971.

Fingarette, Herbert. *The Self in Transformation.* New York, 1963.

Flynn, Thomas. *Sartre and Marxist Existentialism.* Chicago, 1983.

Frederikse, Julie. *South Africa: A Different Kind of War.* Johannesburg, 1986.

Greenberg, Stanley B. *Race and State in Capitalist Development.* New Haven, 1980.

———. *Legitimating the Illegitimate: State, Markets, and Resistance in South Africa.* New Haven, 1987.

Hilberg, Raul. *The Destruction of the European Jews.* New York, 1979.

Kren, George M., and Leon Rappoport. *The Holocaust and the Crisis of Human Behavior.* New York, 1980.

Lelyveld, Joseph. *Move Your Shadow.* New York, 1985.

Lipton, Merle. *Capitalism and Apartheid.* Aldershot, England, 1985.

Lodge, Tom. *Black Politics in South Africa Since 1945.* London, 1983.

Louw-Potgieter, Joha. *Afrikaner Dissidents: A Social Psychological Study of Identity and Dissent.* Clevedon, England, 1988.

Magubane, Bernard Makhosezwe. *The Political Economy of Race and Class in South Africa.* New York, 1979.

Magubane, Bernard, and Ibbo Mandaza, eds. *Whither South Africa?* Trenton, N. J., 1988.

Mandela, Nelson. *The Struggle Is My Life.* New York, 1986.

Marcuse, Herbert. *The Aesthetic Dimension.* Boston, 1978.

Milgram, Stanley. *Obedience to Authority.* New York, 1974.

Moerdijk, Donald. *Anti-development: South Africa and Its Bantustans.* Paris, 1981.

Moodie, T. Dunbar. *The Rise of Afrikanerdom.* Berkeley, 1975.

Morris, Mike, and Vishnu Padayachee. "State Reform Policy in South Africa." *Transformation* 7 (1988).

Murray, Martin. *South Africa: Time of Agony, Time of Destiny.* London, 1987.

Nolutshungu, Sam C. *Changing South Africa.* Cape Town, 1983.

Nupen, M. A. "Philosophy and the Crisis in South Africa," *Transformation* 7 (1988).

O'Meara, Dan. *Volkskapitalisme: Class, Capital, and Ideology in the Development of Afrikaner Nationalism, 1934–1948.* Cambridge, 1983.

Orkin, Mark. *The Struggle and the Future: What Black South Africans Really Think.* Johannesburg, 1986.

Phillips, Ian. "Negotiation and Armed Struggle in Contemporary South Africa." *Transformation* 6 (1988).

Rodney, Walter. *How Europe Underdeveloped Africa.* Washington, D.C., 1982.

Rogers, Barbara. *Divide and Rule: South Africa's Bantustans.* London, 1980.

Sartre, Jean-Paul. *Antisemite and Jew.* New York, 1948.

———. *Being and Nothingness.* New York, 1956.

———. *Critique of Dialectical Reason,* I. London, 1976.

———. *The Emotions: Outline of a Theory.* New York, 1948.

———. Preface to Frantz Fanon, *The Wretched of the Earth.* New York, 1968.

Saul, John S., and Stephen Gelb. *Crisis in South Africa.* New York, 1981.

Seedat, Aziza. *Crippling a Nation: Health in Apartheid South Africa.* London, 1984.

Simkins, Charles. *Reconstructing South African Liberalism.* Johannesburg, 1986.

Simons, H. J., and R. E. Simons. *Class and Color in South Africa.* Harmondsworth, 1969.

Simson, Howard. *The Social Origins of Afrikaner Fascism and Its Apartheid Policy.* Stockholm, 1980.

Sunter, Clem. *The World and South Africa in the 1990s.* Cape Town, 1987.

Tatum, Lyle, ed. *South Africa: Challenge and Hope.* New York, 1987.

Thompson, Leonard. *The Political Mythology of Apartheid.* New Haven, 1985.

Thompson, Leonard, and Andrew Prior. *South African Politics.* New Haven, 1982.

Turner, Richard. *The Eye of the Needle.* Maryknoll, N.Y., 1978.

Unterhalter, Elaine. *Forced Removal: The Division, Segregation, and Control of the People of South Africa.* London, 1987.

Wallerstein, Immanuel. *Historical Capitalism.* London, 1983.

War and Moral Responsibility. Princeton, 1974.